WONDERS
OF THE WORLD

WONDERS
OF THE WORLD

igloo

igloo

First published in 2010
by Igloo Books Ltd
Cottage Farm
Sywell
NN6 0BJ

www.igloo-books.com

A copy of the British Library Cataloguing-in-Publication
Data is available from the British Library

10 9 8 7 6 5 4 3 2

ISBN:978-0-85734-255-3

Written by Martin Howard

Printed and manufactured in China

CONTENTS

INTRODUCTION

Our entire planet is a thing of wonder. Spinning in space, its surface over 70 per cent water, this green-blue gem swirled with white clouds is the only celestial body in the universe known to support life: something it does with flair. Throughout the world's ecosystems, from boiling volcanic vents on the deepest ocean floor to the highest peaks, live millions of species, an incredible profusion that continues to reveal new, never-before-seen plants and animals even today. This abundance of flora and fauna dwells on a world that could have been purposefully created to provide its inhabitants with as many environments as possible; a world that poets might describe as 'sublime.' For the planet Earth is a world of unique landscapes and breathtaking vistas. From scorched wind-sculpted desert sands to humid tropical rainforest. From tumbling rivers and waterfalls, to flower studded meadows, great craggy chasms and subterranean caves. From isolated paradise islands and vivid coral reefs, to frozen terrains of ice and snow, it is a constantly changing world, ever beautiful, and always surprising.

Onto these landscapes humans have imposed their own wonders. From the earliest days of our species' history we have strived to build ever higher and bigger monuments to our own existence and works that defy nature. In the middle of cities and far out in the wildernesses are great pyramids, temples and tombs; vast statues and soaring skyscrapers that seem to break new records every year, bridges and dams that tame the widest and most turbulent stretches of water. While some are inevitably lost to the passage of time – the Pyramids of Giza are now the only remnant of the original Seven Wonders of the World – new wonders continue to define human evolution. Where our ancestors built palaces for the gods, today our triumphs include great laboratories that orbit the planet in space.

Within this book are wonders of all types. Alongside natural marvels such as the Great Barrier Reef, Victoria Falls, volcanoes, iceberg-strewn fjords and the Earth's highest peaks are the most amazing of human achievements of all kinds. From the delicate sculpted-marble filigree of the Taj Mahal to great canals that cut through continents. Presenting a journey through history, and to every corner of the globe, it visits the most awe-inspiring places that planet Earth has to offer.

ABU SIMBEL

Ramesses II was the greatest of Ancient Egyptian pharaohs. During his reign, which spanned seven decades, Egypt expanded and became more prosperous than ever before. Like his predecessors, Ramesses II lavished a large proportion of his wealth on numerous grand building projects, but the most famous – and beautiful – are two temples at Abu Simbel on the western bank of Lake Nasser.

The larger of the two is the Temple of Ramesses, which is considered one of the greatest feats of art and architecture of the ancient world. At the temple's entrance sit four colossal statues of the pharaoh. Alongside the Great Pyramid, the statues are the most instantly recognizable and awe-inspiring legacy of Ancient Egypt. Built to commemorate the pharaoh's 'victory' against the Hittites at the Battle of Kadesh (historians believe the battle was more likely to have been a draw), the temple was directly carved into the rocky mountainside over a 20-year period from roughly 1244 to 1224 BC. The iconic, 20-meter (65-ft) tall, sitting statues guard the entrance, above which stands the falcon-headed god Ra Harakhti. Within is a complex of halls and chambers dominated by the hypostyle hall with its eight massive pillars. Such is the perfection of the construction that twice a year, at the equinoxes of February 22 and October 22, the light of the rising sun pierces deep into the interior of the temple to illuminate three of the four statues of gods there. The fourth statue is of Ptah, god of the underworld, who remains forever in darkness.

The second temple is dedicated to the goddess Hathor, personified by Nefertari, the most favored of Ramesses' 200 wives. Sometimes known as The Small Temple, Nefertari's is no less beautiful for being less monumental in scale. Outside the entrance are 10-meter (33-ft) high statues of the queen and the pharaoh, which are remarkable not only for their beauty but for the fact that Nefertari's statue is the same size as Ramesses'. This is highly unusual as the convention was for the pharaoh to dwarf all those around him – as can be seen on Ramesses' own temple – and is testament to the pharaoh's love for Nefertari.

Inside, the temple is a simplified version of its larger neighbor, with many exquisite carvings showing Nefertari and Ramesses making offerings to the gods.

Following their completion the temples fell into disuse as the centuries passed and were eventually swallowed by rising sands. In 1813, however, a Swiss traveler named J. L. Bruckhardt was led to the site by a young local boy (who, legend has, it was the Abu Simbel for whom the site was named) and found the larger temple's top frieze of 20 carved baboons. Bruckhardt passed word of the discovery on to the Italian explorer Giovanni Belzoni, who managed to dig away enough sand to enter the temple in 1817. Both temples were dismantled and moved between 1964 and 1968 to save them from being inundated by the rising waters that would result after the construction of the Aswan High Dam. Now a protected UNESCO World Heritage Site, the temples of Abu Simbel are among Egypt's most popular tourist attractions and, over 3,000 years after they were built, still elicit awe and wonder from visitors.

Main image: *The exterior of The Small Temple, dedicated to Queen Nefertari and the goddess Hathor, boasts exquisite carvings of the pharaoh and his most beloved wife.*

Inset: *The four statues of Ramesses II that adorn the entrance of the Great Temple of Abu Simbel.*

ACROPOLIS OF ATHENS

Although there are numerous other acropoleis in Greece, all fade into insignificance beside the Athenian Acropolis. Indeed, such is its scale, magnificence and fame that it is usually known simply as 'The Acropolis.' Crowned by the Parthenon, the site contains many other relics of supreme cultural, architectural and archeological importance and is undoubtedly the greatest legacy of the Ancient Greek world.

Rising 150 meters (490 ft) above the modern city, the Acropolis is a flat-topped rock that – like other acropoleis – once served Athens as a defensive stronghold, refuge in times of strife and a sacred sanctuary. The term *acropolis* translates as 'upper city' and such places were common in the ancient Greek city-states where wars were frequent. In myth, it is the site where the goddess Athena and the god Poseidon challenged each other to become the city's patron. Athena won, and the city was named in her honor. The Erechtheum was built on the spot where she is said to have made an olive tree grow by touching a spear to the earth.

What sets the Athenian Acropolis apart is the scale and quality of its structures, most of which date to around the 5th century BC. Although there are many archeological remains that show the hill was of great importance to Athenians from the city's very earliest days, many of its buildings (including an older Parthenon) were destroyed by Persia in 480 BC.

After the Athenians repulsed the invaders, the city became the most important of the Greek city-states. In 460 BC, a 30-year 'Golden Age' began, during which many of the great temples that still top the Acropolis were built (often using the remains of older structures in their foundations). Under the guidance of the Athenian sculptor Pheidias and two architects – Ictinus and Callicrates – the most famous buildings of the Acropolis took shape, perfect examples of the Classical architectural style that has inspired countless architects since.

At the entrance to the Acropolis stands the remains of a huge gateway that was designed in perfect harmony with the Parthenon. Known as the Propylaea, the stairway up to it marked the final steps of the Sacred Way, which stretched to Eleusis, about 20 kilometers (12 miles) northwest of Athens. The most celebrated of the Acropolis' buildings is, of course, the Parthenon. When finished in 438 BC the massive building housed a great bronze statue of Athena. The roof was supported by 46 outer and 19 inner columns and at each end featured a fabulously sculpted pediment that depicted scenes of Athena being born from the head of Zeus (eastern pediment) and her contest with Poseidon (western pediment). Elsewhere on the site are the remains of other temples, sanctuaries and theaters that – though now ruined to a lesser or greater extent – still retain something of the glory of Classical Athens.

Main image: *Standing high above the city, the Athenian Acropolis served as a sanctuary, religious center and treasury.*

Inset: *On the north side of the Acropolis is the Erechtheum temple with its famous porch supported by the toga-draped female figures known as Caryatids.*

Following pages: *Long held to be an architectural wonder, the Parthenon's design incorporated subtle optical illusions that increased its appearance of symmetry.*

AKASHI-KAIKYO BRIDGE

The longest suspension bridge in the world and a marvel of modern engineering, Japan's Akashi-Kaikyo Bridge prompted the development of new construction innovations that have unlocked the possibility of even longer bridges.

Opened in 1998 and also known as the Pearl Bridge, the Akashi-Kaikyo Bridge connects the main Japanese island of Honshu to the island of Shikoku. With the central span measuring 1,991 meters (6,532 ft), it is longer than the world's other great suspension bridges by some considerable distance. The previous record holder was Denmark's StoreBaelt Bridge, which was opened the same year and is

366 meters (1,200 ft) shorter, while the Akashi-Kaikyo is longer than San Francisco's famous Golden Gate Bridge by 710 meters (2,329 ft).

In designing the bridge, architects and engineers not only had to contend with the unprecedented span, but with the site's numerous individual difficulties. The Akashi Strait is a dangerous stretch of water; in fact, the idea of building a bridge was first advanced after two ferries sank there in 1955 with the loss of many lives, including 168 children. High winds and violent storms are common and the Akashi Strait's tidal currents reach a fierce 4.5 meters (15 ft) per second. The region

is also prone to earthquakes. Indeed, an earthquake struck during construction, moving the towers so much that the bridge is about 1 meter (3 ft) longer than originally intended. These challenges were met with great leaps forward in building techniques. After lengthy testing (which involved the building of the world's biggest wind tunnel) many innovative systems and materials were used during the bridge's decade-long construction. These included a new type of concrete, which was used for the foundations, as well as plates beneath the bridge and a unique girder-stiffening system that were devised to cope with high wind speeds. The suspension cables were specially manufactured and each is made up of 36,830 wires that stretch continuously from one anchorage to another. Each cable has a diameter of 1.12 meters (44 in). Pendulums were also built in and help to control vibration; the bridge is able to expand by up to 2 meters (6 ft 6 in) per day.

The result is an elegantly designed bridge that can withstand an 8.5-Richter magnitude earthquake with an epicenter only 150 kilometers (90 miles) away and gusts of up to 286 kilometers per hour (178 mph). Its two towers rise to a height of 298 meters (978 ft).

Main image: *The Akashi-Kaikyo Bridge in Japan is the world's longest suspension bridge, measuring 1,991 meters (6,532 ft).*

Inset: *Completed in 1998 at a cost of US$3.6 billion (500 billion Japanese Yen), the bridge is now crossed by an average of 23,000 cars each day.*

ALETSCH GLACIER

Some 20,000 years ago 30 per cent of the Earth's surface was hidden beneath great moving sheets of ice thousands of meters thick and with the power to shape entire landscapes. The last ice age ended roughly 12,000 years ago, but remnants of that period of icy grandeur can still be found around the globe. Located in the spectacular Jungfrau-Aletsch-Bietschhorn region of the European Alps, the Aletsch Glacier is the largest on the Eurasian continent and one of the most stunning of the world's remaining glaciers.

The Aletsch is formed at the confluence of three smaller glaciers at Concordia high in the eastern Bernese Alps in Switzerland. From there, it bends and loops for about 23 kilometers (14 miles) between alpine peaks, with an average width of 1.5 kilometers (1 mile) and a total surface area of 120 square kilometers (45 sq miles). The vast mass of compacted snow and ice flows down toward the Rhone Valley at a speed of about 180 meters (590 ft) per year and ends at a height of approximately 1,560 meters (5,118 ft) above sea level. Here, the leading edge thins and the Massa River springs from the glacier's melt water to tumble through gorges and eventually feed the River Rhone. Roughly a kilometer thick at its deepest

point, at the time of the last ice age the glacier would have completely covered the surrounding terrain with only the very highest of peaks poking above its surface. It has been calculated that, if melted, the Aletsch Glacier would provide a liter of water a day for every person on Earth for six years.

A simple recitation of statistics and facts, however, cannot do justice to the glacier's magnificence, or that of the surrounding scenery. With the great river of ice at its center, the region is held to be one of the world's most outstanding areas of natural beauty. Horn peaks and sheer curtains of rock tower above glacial lakes and U-shaped valleys that support a great variety of flora and fauna. The highest summits of the Bernese Alps all overlook the glacier.

The Aletsch Glacier is also of considerable scientific importance, offering insights into glacial history and ongoing processes, such as the changes that occur in the ecosystem as it retreats, as well as the impact of climate change. The glacier has been retreating steadily since the mid-19th century, but over the past few decades the average speed of retreat has increased greatly, not withstanding a few years when it has actually increased in length.

The glacier was designated a UNESCO World Heritage Site in 2001 and is well maintained and protected. It is as popular now with hikers, artists and tourists as it has been for hundreds of years.

Main image: *The Aletsch Glacier, the largest in the Western Eurasia, covers an area of approximately 120 square kilometers (45 sq miles) and moves gradually southeast at an unhurried 180 meters (590 ft) a year.*

Inset: *A breathtaking view through a passage in the ice at the Aletsch Glacier. Sadly, climate change is affecting the coverage of the glacier.*

ALHAMBRA

detail with stunning effect. Deceptively simple in their external appearance, the buildings' designs are Islamic in origin yet unique to this Spanish outpost of the Caliphate.

The Alhambra is located on the crest of the Assabica hill to the southeast of the Spanish city of Granada. Described in Moorish poetry as 'a pearl set among emeralds' the hill was surrounded by forest and the buildings were originally painted white, though *alhambra* means 'the red one' and derives from the region's red clay, of which bricks for the buildings were made. The first of the buildings to occupy the site was the Alcazaba, which dates to the 9th century and is a stern fortress built on the edge of the plateau. It is now mostly in ruins, but beyond it lie the true wonders of the Alhambra: the palaces and gardens of Spain's later Moorish rulers. The first

Built during the reign of the Muslim Moorish Emirs in Al-Andalusia, Spain, the Alhambra is an exceptional complex of buildings that combine rich architectural and ornamental

Moorish king to make his home here was Mohammed I in the 13th century, and over the following centuries – until the region was conquered by Spain's Catholic monarchs, King Ferdinand II of Aragon and Queen Isabella I of Castile in 1492 – his successors added buildings of outstanding beauty, using light and water in an attempt to create Paradise on Earth. Notable among them are the Comares Palace, with its impressive tower, The Palace of the Lions, and the great gates that lead into the complex.

There was no overall plan for the development of the site, and the buildings of the Alhambra proper (some later structures such as the Church of Santa Maria were constructed after Moorish rule ended) were built in something of a jumble and connected by corridors and courtyards. Through great gateways are columned arcades that lead onto magnificent courts such as the Court of the Lions, which is paved with white marble and walled with blue, yellow and gold tiles and enameling. Delicate filigree work is in abundance and, in the center, stands the beautiful white marble Fountain of Lions. Elsewhere are the beautifully decorated harems, once home

to the emir's (king's) wives and consorts, grand audience halls, administration spaces and gardens once filled with orange trees, myrtles and carefully cultivated roses. Streams and fountains would have filled the emir's ears with the soothing sound of running water, as well as helping to cool the air, while light and shadow were delicately used to create ornamental effects.

Sadly, the Alhambra suffered centuries of neglect and thoughtless remodeling after the Moors were defeated, though what remains is a testament to the exquisite artistry of its, mainly Christian and Jewish, builders. It is now a UNESCO World Heritage Site, and one of Spain's most popular tourist attractions.

Main image: *From afar the Alhambra is an imposing, though plain, looking collection of buildings. Its true splendor becomes apparent at close quarters.*

Inset: *The Court of Lions is the main courtyard of the Alhambra and is ornately decorated with filigree walls, a domed roof and 124 white, marble pillars.*

AMAZON BASIN

Covering an area of 7,044,500 square kilometers (2,720,000 sq miles), the Amazon River Basin is the largest of its kind in the world, and also one of the world's most precious, and mysterious, ecosystems. Covering about a third of the South American continent, an incredibly rich profusion of flora and fauna exists beneath the almost unbroken canopy of its dense tropical rainforest. Within an area of 1.3 square kilometers (half a sq mile), 117 different species of tree alone have been counted. As yet, the region is largely unexplored and deep within the forest it is thought that there may be a large number of plant and animal species that non-native humans have never before encountered.

The Amazon Basin is bordered by the rocky Guina Shield to the north, the Central Brazilian Plateau to the south and the Andes to the west. It forms the drainage basin of the Amazon River, and its 15,000 tributaries, and is roughly 6,750 kilometers (4,195 miles) long. Within this sparsely populated and almost unimaginably vast area is the world's largest rainforest. Thought to date back at least 100 million years, the forest experiences constant warm temperatures, which average 30º–35ºC (86º–95ºF) during the day and 20º–25ºC (68º–77ºF) at night and an average 2 meters (80 in) of rainfall each year. These conditions nurture a dizzying abundance of life, the richest ecosystem on the planet.

The Amazon River itself is immense. Second only to the Nile in length, in terms of volume it is without compare. At its mouth, which is 400 kilometers (250 miles) across, 30 trillion liters (8 trillion gallons) of water pour into the Atlantic Ocean, 60 times the output of the Nile. At points along its length it reaches 56 kilometers (35 miles) in width and it is,

itself, teeming with species found nowhere else on Earth. Its deep waters are home to the biggest non-ocean fish in the world – the arapaima, which can grow up to 4.5 meters (15 ft) in length – as well as piranha, electric eels and the world's biggest snake, the anaconda, which spends most of its time in the water.

In recent years, the world has become aware of the great dangers presented to the Amazon Rainforest by deforestation. Among the unique plant species that live here, there are many that have already covered extremely valuable to science and medicine; It is impossible to say what might be lost to humankind if the destruction of the rainforest continues. As the world continues to grow and exploit the planet's ecosystems, it is to be hoped that the Amazon Basin, and its natural riches, will remain a pristine wilderness area and that its many undiscovered wonders will gradually be revealed.

Main image: *The sun sets over the upper canopy of the rainforest in the Amazon Basin.*

Inset: *Trees take root and vines hang over the inchartered waters of the Amazon River in Brazil.*

AMBOSELI NATIONAL PARK

over 400 bird species, such as martial eagle, African fish eagle, pygmy falcon, pelican, kingfisher and bee eater. Another 'gift' from Kilimanjaro is the ever-present dust, which is actually 1,000 year-old volcanic dust deposited from the mountain.

Amboseli was discovered by the wider world relatively late, as the native Maasai people were fierce, proud warriors and few explorers dared set foot in their lands. In fact, the first European to see the area was Joseph Thompson, in 1883, and he was amazed at the abundant wildlife and the swamps that provide a great contrast to the dusty grassland and dried up Pleistocene lake. His wonder has since been shared by Ernest Hemingway, who immortalized the region in literature with his tales of big game hunting here, as well as countless film crews, photographers, documentary makers and tourists. Amboseli is now one of Africa's most popular attractions, though the Maasai still live here. The park is dotted with manyatta, reminders of the traditional Masaai way of life. These dwellings were constructed from bent branches and sealed with cow dung, which would be built quickly and abandoned when grazing became thin and the herds were moved to fresh pastures.

A national park since 1974 and a UNESCO Biosphere Reserve since 1991, Amboseli's beauties are now protected and eco-tourism is carefully managed to preserve the park and benefit the indigenous people.

Just 392 square kilometers (151 sq miles) in size, Amboseli is one of Africa's smaller national parks, yet its incomparable scenery and rich ecosystem combine to make it the most unique. With the cloud-shrouded Mount Kilimanjaro dominating every view and herds of free-roaming zebra, wildebeest and elephant, its landscape is the Africa of popular imagination.

Amboseli is in the Rift Valley Province of Kenya, 260 kilometers (160 miles) from the capital of Nairobi, on the border of Tanzania; in the local Maasai language its name means 'place of water.' Although at first glance it appears to be an arid landscape of grassland and cracked earth, punctuated by gnarled acacia trees, water is actually plentiful here. Despite a low average annual rainfall of just 35 centimeters (14 in), melting snow from the summit of Kilimanjaro is filtered through the volcanic rock and constantly feeds underground rivers which, in turn, supply springs and a system of lush swamps at the mountain's base. The endless water supply has resulted in a delicately balanced ecosystem that supports a bewildering array of wildlife. There are over 50 species of large animal – including impala, lion, giraffe, rhinoceros, cheetah, leopard, caracal and serval cat, as well as the great elephant herds – and

---

Main image: *Mount Kilimanjaro, the highest independent mountain in the world, dominates the skyline of Kenya's Amboseli National Park.*

Inset: *A family of elephants trek through the green marshlands of Amboseli. Elephants have flourished here since the ban on ivory smuggling was introduced.*

ANGKOR WAT

Writing in the late 16th century, one of the first Europeans to set eyes on Angkor Wat – a Portuguese monk by the name of Antonio da Magdalena – said that the temple in what is modern-day Cambodia 'is of such extraordinary construction that it is not possible to describe it with a pen, particularly since it is like no other building in the world. It has towers and decoration and all the refinements which the human genius can conceive of.' He is not the only person to have been awe-struck by the building. Almost half a millennium later Angkor Wat is a World Heritage Site and its graceful harmony, delicate architecture and superb ornamentation continue to amaze and delight hundreds of thousands of foreign visitors each year. The Cambodian people are so proud of the structure that its image now forms part of their flag.

The Angkor Wat temple complex – comprising a wide moat, enclosing wall and the temple proper – was commissioned by King Suryavarman II early in the 12th century. Its name translates as 'city temple' and it is situated just outside the old capital of Baphuon, in an area that is renowned for its ancient buildings. It was dedicated to the Hindu god Vishnu (though in the late 13th century the country converted to Buddhism and built many Buddhist dedications on top of the original hindu designs) is thought to have been designed as Suryavarman's last resting place. If so, it is a funerary complex to rival the pyramids of Egypt.

Opposite page: *Built during the reign of King Suryavarman II in the early 12th century, Angkor Wat was the main temple of the Hindu god Vishnu, but converted to Buddhism in the late 13th century.*

Right: *Although there are ongoing international efforts to restore the temple of Angkor Wat, much of the site has suffered from neglect. Here, giant tree roots have grown around parts of the structure.*

Following pages: *An aerial view of the Angkor Wat Temple complex.*

The temple has lent its name to a style of architecture – the Angkor Wat Style. The structure is mostly of sandstone blocks, so perfectly placed that it is often difficult to find the seams. The main temple itself rises from a terrace in three rectangular galleries, the inner two of which feature four towers in the shape of lotus buds. A lofty central tower completes the quincunx (four geometric points with a fifth at the center). The structure is richly ornamented on almost every surface with breathtaking bas-reliefs (low reliefs) that detail ancient battles and scenes from Hindu literature and mythology, while the walls are decorated with images of guardian spirits.

Surrounding the temple is a 4.5-meter (15-ft) high wall which encloses an area of 820,000 square meters (203 acres) and is punctuated by towered gopuras (entrance structures). The wall, its towers, and grand gateways are, again, richly decorated with carvings and bas-reliefs and are in perfect harmony with the architecture of the inner temple.

Angkor Wat has been sacked, neglected and subjected to poor restoration work over its long history, but the surrounding moat has kept the encroaching jungle at bay and it has never fallen into disuse. Today, its popularity as a tourist destination helps fund an ongoing restoration and protection program.

ARC DE TRIOMPHE

Commissioned by Napoleon Bonaparte after the Battle of Austerlitz, the Arc de Triomphe is one of the most dramatic works of architecture to be found in any of the world's great cities.

To be exact, its proper name is the Arc de Triomphe de l'Étoile. Another arch – the less impressive Arc de Triomphe du Carrousel – can be found close by. It is located at the center of the Place Charles de Gaulle (commonly known as the Place de l'Étoile) in Paris from which radiate no less than 16 of the city's grand, straight boulevards. This means that the arch seems visible from almost everywhere in central Paris, and it forms an impressive backdrop to the cityscape. At 50 meters (164 ft) high, 45 meters (148 ft) broad, and 22 meters (72 ft) deep, it is the second largest triumphal arch in existence. So large that in 1919, after a parade to celebrate the end of World War I, the aviator Charles Godefroy was able to fly a biplane through it.

Architecturally, the arch is Classical in design and resembles the triumphal arches of the Roman Empire, though in ornament it surely outstrips its forebears. It was designed in 1806 by Jean Chalgrin (who died in 1811 and was succeeded by various architects until construction was finally completed almost 30 years after earth was broken) and is adorned with friezes that were created by some of France's finest sculptors. The scenes commemorate all French wars, though particularly those of Napoleon, and bear names such as Resistance and Peace, The Triumph of 1810 and Departure of the Volunteers of 1792. Its inner walls are inscribed with the names of First French Empire generals – those who died in battle are underlined – while columns bear the names of Bonaparte's victorious battles. An attic contains a superb frieze depicting French soldiers, above which are 30 shields that list victories of the Revolution and Napoleonic wars.

Beneath the arch are vaults and the famous Tomb of the Unknown Soldier, who was interred on Armistice Day, 1920. An eternal flame burns in the tomb, keeping alive the memory of all those who perished and remained unidentified in World War I (and also World War II). Each year, on November 11, a solemn remembrance ceremony is held here.

During the two centuries that the Arc de Triomphe has graced the Paris skyline, it has seen numerous victory parades and marches, by conquerors and allies as well as French armies. Today, it reminds each new generation of locals and tourists of French glories past and remains one of the most striking features of one of the world's most beautiful cities.

Opposite page: *Standing at the end of the Champs-Élysées, the French capital's most famous thoroughfare, the Arc de Triomphe commemorates the soldiers who fought for France, particularly during the Napoleonic Wars.*

Left: *One of the many impressive sculptures that adorn the Arc de Triomphe. Entitled The Triumph of Napoleon it was sculpted by Jean-Pierre Cortot.*

MOUNT ATHOS

Hidden away on a picturesque mountain peninsula in Macedonia is a small world; a world that is totally unfamiliar to the one most of us know. Mount Athos is the home of a tiny, self-governed state where even time moves differently. Here, the days are still counted on the Julian calendar and the hours by the Byzantine system, which begins at sunset rather than midnight. No women are allowed and the days are spent observing a strict monastic timetable. It is a holy place, populated almost entirely by monks living within the 20 historic monasteries that cling to the mountain's slopes and small isolated communities called *sketes*.

The peninsula itself is a 60-kilometer (37-mile) strip of land that, though joined to the mainland, can only be reached by boat. It is dominated by the thickly forested Mount Athos, which reaches a height of 2,033 meters (6,670 ft). Only men are allowed on shore and even then they have to have a special visa, signed by four of the monastic secretaries. Those pilgrims and visitors who are lucky enough to reach the peninsula find, on Mount Athos, a place of peace and tranquility dotted with historic buildings that contain treasures of medieval art.

In fact, Mount Athos has a history that stretches back to the very beginnings of Christianity. The monks' legends tell that the Virgin Mary landed here when a ship that was carrying her to Cyprus was blown off course. Christ's mother was so delighted by the mountain's beauty that she prayed that it might become her garden. A reply came in the form of a disembodied voice, which told her that the mountain would be her inheritance and a refuge for those seeking salvation.

By the 4th century AD, Mount Athos had, indeed, become a sanctuary for Christians, though historical records from that time are scant and, in those times, pagans also inhabited the peninsula. The first monastic communities and monasteries appeared in the 9th century and, by 943, the state's borders had been set and the Xiropotamou monastery was growing in size. The year 958 saw the arrival of a monk called Athanasios the Athonite who founded the Great Lavra monastery.

Over the following centuries, the monks of Mount Athos prospered. More monasteries were built (the last of the 20 was the Stavronikita monastery, which dates to the 16th century) and remained largely untouched by world events, though the fall of the Byzantine Empire and the rise of the region's new power, the Muslim Ottoman Empire, saw the small community taxed heavily.

Today, life on Mount Athos goes on as it has for centuries; the monks worship, work and rest in almost total isolation from the rest of the world. Their monasteries and the great trove of artworks and documents they have accumulated over a thousand years are now a protected UNESCO World Heritage Site.

Main image: *The lush green slopes of Mount Athos, on the Halkidiki peninsula, rise to 2,033 meters (6,670 ft).*

Inset: *Stavronikita monastery was the last to be consecrated on Mount Athos, in 1536. It is dedicated to Saint Nicholas and is home to about 40 monks.*

AYUTTHAYA

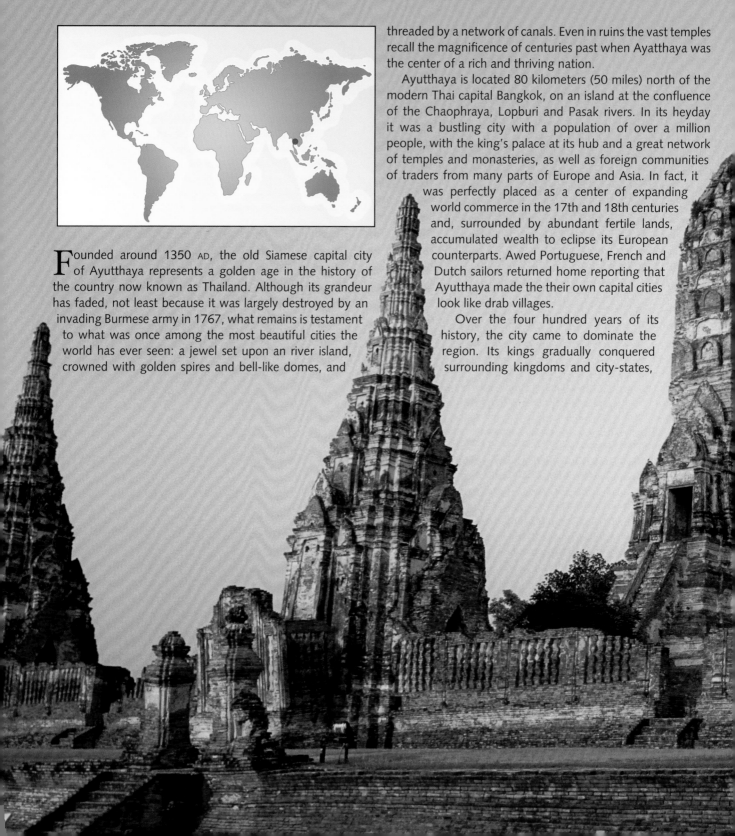

threaded by a network of canals. Even in ruins the vast temples recall the magnificence of centuries past when Ayatthaya was the center of a rich and thriving nation.

Ayutthaya is located 80 kilometers (50 miles) north of the modern Thai capital Bangkok, on an island at the confluence of the Chaophraya, Lopburi and Pasak rivers. In its heyday it was a bustling city with a population of over a million people, with the king's palace at its hub and a great network of temples and monasteries, as well as foreign communities of traders from many parts of Europe and Asia. In fact, it was perfectly placed as a center of expanding world commerce in the 17th and 18th centuries and, surrounded by abundant fertile lands, accumulated wealth to eclipse its European counterparts. Awed Portuguese, French and Dutch sailors returned home reporting that Ayutthaya made the their own capital cities look like drab villages.

Over the four hundred years of its history, the city came to dominate the region. Its kings gradually conquered surrounding kingdoms and city-states,

Founded around 1350 AD, the old Siamese capital city of Ayutthaya represents a golden age in the history of the country now known as Thailand. Although its grandeur has faded, not least because it was largely destroyed by an invading Burmese army in 1767, what remains is testament to what was once among the most beautiful cities the world has ever seen: a jewel set upon an river island, crowned with golden spires and bell-like domes, and

and it spilled over the walled island and into the surrounding countryside as its power and wealth grew. The maps of European merchants of the 18th century show Ayutthaya as a city glowing with gold-leaf encrusted palaces and swarming with fleets of merchant ships.

It is here that the distinctively Thai building style evolved. Many of Ayutthaya's older buildings were built with the towering *prangs* (finger-like spires) of the older Khmer style, while later buildings were crowned with the bell-shaped *chedi* (a domed-shaped stupa). The temple of Wat Phra Si Sanphet, which is at what would have been the heart of the city, is the most famous of Ayutthaya's remains. Its three *chedis* provide a glimpse of the old city's wonders. Other ruins are dotted around the island and surrounding landscape and a few relics of Ayutthaya's past glory remain, such as the large bronze Buddha that was

once enshrined at the Grand Palace and is now at the Viharn Phra Mongkol Bopit building.

Despite its ruined state, Ayutthaya is still recognized as a trove of architectural wonders and a place of great historical interest. It became a UNESCO World Heritage Site in 1991.

Main image: *The Buddhist temple of Wat Chai Watthanaram was built in 1630 by King Prasat Thong. During the Burmese invasion of 1767, the temple was sacked and many of the Buddha statues beheaded.*

Inset: *The pagodas, or chedis, of Wat Phra Si Sanphet were built in the grounds of the royal palace to hold the remains of three ancient kings.*

BANAUE RICE TERRACES

Clinging to the precipitous slopes in the region of Ifugao, on the northern island of Luzon in the Philippines, are hundreds of manmade agricultural terraces that represent one of the greatest building projects of the ancient world. Appearing from afar to resemble giant stairways up the Cordilleras mountains, or map contours carved into the landscape, the terraces ascend to a height of 1,500 meters (4,920 ft), covering an area of 10,360 square kilometers (4,000 sq miles).

The terraces were created between 2,000 and 3,000 years ago and have been maintained and restored by the local people ever since. Using only primitive tools, the Ifugao farmers made them by building restraining walls, creating a series of stepped fields that followed the contours of the mountainside. This amazing achievement was capped with the building of a gravity-powered irrigation system that brought water from springs and streams in the forested peaks above. Held by many to be the Eighth Wonder of the World, the amount of labor needed to build the terraces is comparable to that needed for the construction of the pyramids of Giza. If placed end to end, they would stretch 22,400 kilometers (13,919 miles), or half the way around the globe.

There are no records of exactly when building work began or where the people who made them came from, though there is evidence to suggest that they probably originated in China. In 2105 BC, a tribe known as the Miao rebelled against the Emperor Yu the Great but were beaten by imperial troops and the survivors forced into exile across the sea to the Philippines. The Miao were a mountain people who are known to have cultivated rice. They would have adapted easily to life in the Cordilleras and assimilated into the indigenous peoples, teaching them their agricultural techniques. Over the following years, the combination of the two peoples produced a distinct culture with a set of rituals that centered around the cultivation and consumption of rice. Numerous festivities around the year celebrated the planting and harvesting of crops with the eating of rice cakes and drinking of rice beer.

Today, though some of the terraces are showing signs of erosion, they are still worked in a fashion that has hardly changed since the fields were originally constructed. The Banaue Rice Terraces were designated a UNESCO World Heritage Site in 1995 and, as well as continuing to farm their ancestral lands, the local people now welcome thousands of tourists each year.

Main image: *Over 2,000 years since they were made, the Banaue Rice Terraces are still used to grow rice as well as vegetables.*

Inset: *From above, the terraces present a striking patchwork of steps. However, since they require constant repair work, the condition of some terraces are deteriorating.*

BLACK FOREST

Germany's Black Forest has a reputation for enchantment that stretches back centuries. In fact, logging has thinned the trees and today its pine woodlands are more beautiful than dark, but they do have a unique flavor. Studded with charming villages and towns filled with fine examples of traditional architecture and criss-crossed by streams and ancient trails, the Black Forest is steeped in German heritage.

The Black Forest occupies the southwestern corner of Germany close to the borders of France and Switzerland and covers an almost rectangular area of 12,000 square kilometers (4,600 sq miles). It has a length from north to south of about 200 kilometers (124 miles) and an east to west width of 60 kilometers (37 miles). Once blanketed by glaciers, the forest has numerous peaks of over 1,200 meters (3,937 ft) – the tallest is Feldberg at 1,493 meters (4,898 ft) – while its deep valleys and hanging lakes are reminders of the last ice age. The forest is also the source of the mighty Danube, Europe's

Named for the murky depths of its thick woods, which are made darker still by the shadows of hills and mountains, and long associated with wild fairy tales and looming castles,

second longest river as well as other, smaller, rivers including the Enz, the Kinzig and the Neckar. The dense woodland is mostly made up of pine and fir trees (logging was for centuries an important local industry, giving rise to the prominence of woodcutters in the tales that the region inspired), and is home to numerous species of wildlife. Some, such as bears and wolves, are now gone, though reintroduction programs are underway. However, the forest is still home to wild boar as well as deer and many species of bird.

As well as logging, the Black Forest was also once famous for its silver mines, which made the region wealthy, while the town of Freiberg became a renowned seat of learning. Its city hall, fantastic turreted city gates and 16th century Merchants Hall are superb examples of the local architectural style, while other towns and villages such as Calw, Gengenbach and Schiltach are redolent of Germany's past with their dark-beamed houses and steeply-pitched roof lines.

Mining dwindled during the 17th century and the Black Forest subsequently became known as a center of clock and watch making, an industry that thrives today, delighting tourists with shops full of the area's famous cuckoo clocks. All logging is strictly monitored to make sure that as many trees are planted as cut down, and tourism is now the Black Forest's primary industry. Many of the old mines, which, legend has it, were worked by dwarves, are now open to the public. As famous for its rich cakes and black ham as it is for its superb scenery, the Black Forest remains one of Europe's most magical corners.

Main image: *Sunset over the Black Forest as seen from the Schwarzwaldhochstrasse mountain pass. The dense woodland inspired many folktales about witches, werewolves and dwarves.*

Inset: *Within the forest are beautiful old towns and villages, such as Gengenbach that have changed little over the centuries.*

BLUE MOUNTAINS

the Blue Mountains have never been short of admirers, but perhaps the greatest compliment the area has ever received came from the lips of Charles Darwin. During a visit to Grose Valley, history's most celebrated naturalist described the scenery he found there as 'Stupendous… magnificent.'

Inhabited by Australian Aboriginals for roughly 22,000 years, as attested to by carvings and the famous hand stencils at a site now known as the Red Hands Cave, the mountains were first seen by European colonists in the late 18th century. The first governor of New South Wales, Arthur Philip, gave them the rather unwieldy name of the Carmarthen and Landowne Hills, and for a number of years the range was thought to be impassable by Australia's new settlers (which was seen as fortuitous as it stopped convicts escaping in that direction), though the Aboriginals, in fact, used two routes through them.

The foothills begin 50 kilometers (31 miles) west of the city of Sydney in Australia's New South Wales territory and the peaks and plateaux extend westward to Coxs River, rising to a height of 1,190 meters (3,904 ft). The characteristic sheer sandstone cliffs were formed by erosion of wind and water over millions of years. Gorges, some many hundreds of meters deep – the deepest is 760 meters (2,493 ft) – cut through the range and in some cases harbor rare temperate rainforest. At higher levels, the plateaux are draped with eucalyptus forest, punctuated with hanging swamps, and within isolated valleys it is possible to find Wollemi Pine, as well as other species of plant that have existed in isolation here since before the world'd continents drifted apart. Other features of the stunning scenery include waterfalls and cave systems such as the Jenolan limestone caves. When seen from afar, a distinctive blue haze blankets the mountains and has lent the range a more appropriate name than the one used by Arthur Philip. It is caused by a phenomenon known as 'mie scattering' which occurs when airborne particles interfere with ultraviolet radiation in the sun's rays.

In recognition of the outstanding value of its plant life, the Greater Blue Mountains Area, which covers about 10,000 square kilometers (3,900 sq miles) was adopted as a World Heritage Area in 2000. Among its many more modern attractions is the Katooomba Scenic Railway, which was adapted from old mining tracks and is officially the steepest in the world.

Australia's Blue Mountains are not only a unique and spectacular feature of the Australian landscape but are home to some of the world's most precious habitats. The range's swamps, wetlands, grasslands, heaths and plateaux contain species that are found nowhere else on the planet. As rich in natural beauty as they are in botanical wonders,

Main image: *Golden afternoon sunlight on the Three Sisters rock formation in the Blue Mountains.*

Inset: *The spectacular Hanging Rock of Grose Valley in Australia's Blue Mountains.*

Following pages: *Mount Solitary at dawn, as a cloud of mist rolls across the valley.*

BOROBUDUR

The world's largest Buddhist monument, the Borobudur temple is a complex and stunningly beautiful work of architecture built in the shape of a three-dimensional *mandala* (a Buddhist symbol representing the cosmos). Ornamented with thousands of superb reliefs that illustrate the life of Buddha Shakyamuni, and over 500 Buddha statues, it is thought that the entire structure was built to represent Buddhist teachings. As such, it was a place where pilgrims would walk through 3.2 kilometers (2 miles) of corridors and stairways around a giant instructional sermon relating the steps on the journey to nirvana.

Borobudur is located on the Indonesian island of Java about 40 kilometers (25 miles) from the city of Yogyakarta. Well over a thousand years old, its origins are shrouded in mystery. No one knows who built it, or exactly when, and there are no written records of its construction. Archeologists and historians agree, however, that work on the temple is likely to have started in the mid to late 8th century AD and have taken around 75 years to complete.

Architecturally, it is a vast structure with an area of 2,500 square meters (26,900 sq ft) comprising over two million stone blocks. It rises from a square foundation about 118 meters (387 ft) to each side with the lower six of its platforms being square and the highest three circular (the circle is symbolic of a perfect state in Buddhism, and of eternity without beginning or end). The higher platforms feature 72 small, domed buildings known as *stupas*, while a larger *stupa* rises from the very top level. Each of these is pierced with small windows and is home to statues of the Buddha. Around the complex are stairways and corridors that are lined with instructive reliefs, and which would have guided pilgrims up the levels to the summit. Each level represents a stage on the journey to enlightenment.

It is thought that the temple fell into disuse sometime between the 10th and 11th centuries, possibly because political power moved away from the region, or perhaps more likely because nearby volcanoes erupted and showered it with a thick layer of ash. Like the mystery surrounding its construction, no one knows for sure why it was abandoned. What is certain is

that for many centuries, Borobudur's wonders lay forgotten beneath ash and jungle until rediscovered by a Dutch engineer under the command of Java's British governor Thomas Stamford Raffles in 1814. Over the following two decades the site was gradually cleared and, as Borobudur gained worldwide attention, efforts were made restore it. In 1975, the Indonesian government, in partnership with UNESCO, began the largest and most comprehensive of these. Over seven years, hundreds of workers cleaned and strengthened the structure and, in 1991, Borobudur became a UNESCO World Heritage Site. Today, it is Indonesia's most popular tourist attraction.

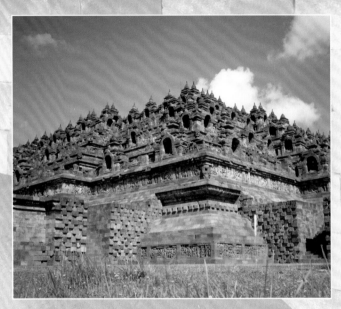

Main image: *Now a World Heritage Site, the Temple of Borobudur was constructed in the 8th century and is the largest Buddhist temple in the world.*

Inset: *There were originally 504 statues of Buddha in the temple. Now 300 are damaged and 43 are missing.*

BURJ KHALIFA

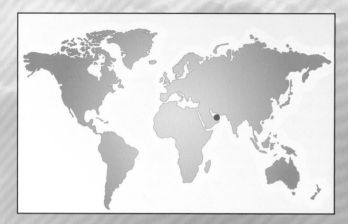

At 828 meters (2,716 ft), Dubai's Burj Khalifa (which translates as Khalifa Tower) is the tallest man-made structure in the world to date. It also holds many other records, including the most floors of any building (160), world's highest observation deck (on the 124th floor) at 442 meters (1,450 ft) above the ground and the world's highest swimming pool (76th floor). So lofty is its spire that it can be seen from over 95 kilometers (60 miles) away.

Burj Khalifa was designed by Skidmore, Owings & Merrill, the company behind some of the world's greatest skyscrapers, such as New York's World Trade Center and Chicago's Sears Tower (now known as Willis Tower), both of which have held the record of the world's tallest building. Its construction presented the architects with numerous problems. Not only had a building of such height never been attempted before, but Dubai is prone to earthquakes, fierce storms and high winds (the top of the tower sways about 2 meters (5 ft) in Dubai's prevailing winds). In fact, the architects designed an entirely new building system known as the 'buttressed core' especially for the tower. This involves a hexagonal core that is held fast by buttresses that form an integral part of the three outer towers. With their innovative design ideas the architects succeeded in designing an incredible – and so far safe –

structure that in appearance is a harmonious blend of Western and Islamic influences.

The open petals of the desert flower Hymenocallis were the inspiration for the tower's base and the skyscraper rises in three petal 'lobes' gathered around a central core arranged in a Y-shape, designed to maximize views out onto the Persian Gulf. Each lobe is of staggered height, which give that pleasing spiraling effect. Behind the shimmering 28,000 panels of reflective glass, stainless steel plating and aluminum of its exterior are over a thousand luxury apartments, 49 floors of offices and space for a 160-room hotel.

Work on the tower began in 2004 and – originally – it was to have been named Burj Dubai, but by the time of its completion a global economic downturn had affected Dubai badly and the state was forced to look to its oil-rich neighbor, Abu Dhabi, for financial assistance. In recognition of the help given, the tower was renamed for the emir of Abu Dhabi, Khalifa bin Zayed Al Nahayan. It was officially opened by Dubai's ruler, Sheikh Mohammed Bin Rashid Al Maktoum on January 4, 2010, amid a fantastic show of fireworks.

Main image: *The world's tallest building, Burj Khalifa, seen towering over the Dubai skyline at sunset.*

Inset: *Fireworks exploding to mark the opening ceremony of the Burj Khalifa in Dubai on January 4, 2010.*

CAPPADOCIA

Located in the east of Anatolia, in the middle of Turkey, the Cappadocia region stretches about 400 kilometers (250 miles) east to west and 250 kilometers (160 miles) north to south. Its highest peak is Mount Ericyes at 3,916 meters (12,847 ft). Formed by volcanic explosions millions of years ago, in some places the relatively soft rock has since been eroded into hundreds of fantastic pillars, often tipped with minaret-like spires, that appear to have been created by human hand. They are, however, entirely natural and lend the landscape its unique splendor. Wind and water are not the only agencies to have carved Cappadocia though. Early humans, who found naturally formed caves that offered protection from animal attacks and rival tribes, exploited the ease with which the rock could be shaped. Over hundreds of years various cultures mined into the rock to create vast subterranean complexes with villages and 'castles' on the surface. Of the latter, the

The Cappadocia region is a place like no other: an extraordinary combination of natural and manmade wonders. Its vast 1,000-meter (3,300-ft) high plateau is scattered with volcanic peaks and the characteristic 'chimneys', eroded by wind and water over millennia, creating a landscape of startling, eerie, beauty. Carved into, and beneath, the rock are extensive underground cities some inhabited by humans since the Bronze Age.

most famous is Uchisar Castle, which is at the highest point of the Cappadocia region and offers stunning panoramic views. There are numerous underground cities (the largest is Derinkuyu), which are formed of chambers hollowed from the rock and connected by intentionally tight passageways. The narrowness allows only one person at a time to pass and would have made it extremely difficult for attackers to storm the caves.

Cappadocia is thought to have once been part of the Hittite Empire (called Hatti during the Bronze Age), and later became part of the Persian Empire under the Great King Darius I. Indeed, the first written reference to the region is to be found in Persian inscriptions dating to the 6th century BC. In the early Christian period Cappadocia's caves, carefully hidden by camouflaged gateways, provided shelter for persecuted Christians. Among the region's most spectacular remains are

monasteries and churches that were once at the heart of the spreading new religion.

Today, Cappadocia's Göreme area is a UNESCO World Heritage Site and a superb place to view the region's many wonders as well as its unique cultural history.

Main image: *The stunning hillsides of Cappadocia are formed of soft volcanic rock. The area is famed for its fairy chimneys (also known as hoodoos) and for the houses, churches and castles that locals have carved into the rock faces.*

Inset: *The highest point in Cappadocia, Uchisar Castle, and its surrounding dwellings were hollowed into the rock, creating rooms, corridors and underground passages. Unfortunately, erosion has taken its toll on the ancient settlement and many areas are now unreachable.*

CHRIST THE REDEEMER

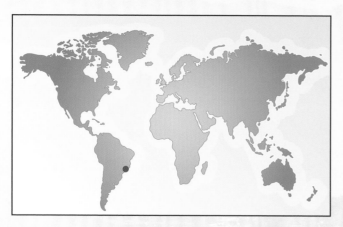

Defining the cityscape of Rio de Janeiro as the Statue of Liberty does New York City, the monumental Christ the Redeemer is one of the world's largest statues and a magnificent example of the Art Deco style of the 1920s and 30s. Looking down over the city from the 710-meter (2,329-ft) peak of Corcovado mountain, the colossal figure is a Brazilian icon and was listed as one of the New Seven Wonders of the World in 2007.

The idea of capping Corcovado's summit with a religious statue was first put forward in the mid-19th century by a Catholic priest named Pedro Maria Boss. Although Brazil's ruling family refused to fund the project at that time, the peak seemed to offer a natural pedestal for a grand monument and Boss's concept proved persistent. In 1889, however, the country became a republic and with the separation of church and state it seemed that funds would never become available to construct a statue that would be large enough to see from the city below. Then, in 1921, the Archdiocese of Rio de Janeiro unexpectedly took up the idea once more and began raising money. Brazilian Catholics responded enthusiastically and the Archdiocese were soon able to start looking at designs, rejecting early proposals for a cross and a statue of Christ with a globe in his hands in favor of a figure of the Savior with arms held wide in welcome.

The chosen design was by Brazilian engineer Heitor da Silva Costa and was finessed, in the Art Deco style, by French sculptor Paul Landowski. Just a year after the fundraising effort had started, construction began. Project engineers settled on making the statue in reinforced concrete and facing it with soapstone (shipped from Sweden), which could endure the fierce weather of the mountain peak, and over the next nine years the colossal figure took shape. Inaugurated during an extravagant ceremony on October 12, 1931, the completed monument stands 39.6 meters (130 ft) tall with a width from fingertip to fingertip of 30 meters (98 ft). The final cost came to US$250,000, about $3.5 million in today's money.

Since it was dedicated, Christ the Redeemer has become one of the country's greatest attractions. Each year, particularly at times of religious significance, many thousands of visitors take the train that travels up the mountain and climb the 220 steps to the statue's base. Their reward is not only an appreciation of the statue's colossal scale, but spectacular views of the Brazilian coast.

Main image: *One of the world's best-known statues, the grand Christ the Redeemer stands atop Corcovado overlooking Rio de Janeiro and Guanabara Bay.*

Inset: *The exquisite statue is widely held to be a symbol of welcome, faith and acceptance in Rio de Janeiro, and throughout Brazil.*

COLOSSEUM

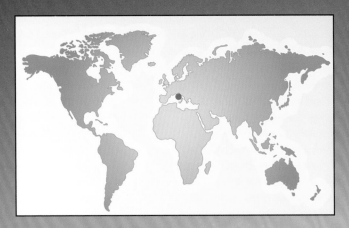

half-ruined Colosseum is a breathtaking structure. Built at the command of emperors and once the stage for lethal gladiatorial contests and the bloody slaying of criminals and Christian martyrs, the Colosseum symbolizes the might of Ancient Rome and is among its crowning architectural achievements.

A short walk to the east of the Forum, in the center of Rome, the Colosseum stands on the site of a great lake and garden built by the Emperor Nero after Rome burned in 64 AD. When Vespasian came to power in 69 AD, he was determined to erase the memory of his hated predecessor and devised the Colosseum as a gift to the people of Rome, making Nero's private pleasure grounds a public arena. Construction began around 70 AD and was finished, under the rule of Titus, a decade later. Complete, the Colosseum – or the Flavian Amphitheater as it was called (Vespasian was the first emperor of the Flavian Dynasty) – stood 189 meters (620 ft) long and 156 meters (511 ft) wide. Its great, arcaded façade rose in three storeys of

O ne of the glories of the Roman Empire, and the greatest amphitheater ever built, even now – in a world where skyscrapers and engineering wonders are commonplace – the

arches to a height of 48 meters (157 ft) and was 545 meters (1,788 ft) in circumference. Inside was tiered seating that could accommodate a crowd of 50,000 with an imperial box to the north and a box for Vestal Virgins to the south. Roman citizens took their seats according to rank, with senators also being allocated special seating, above which sat nobles and the wealthy. Ordinary citizens sat at the highest levels, furthest from the action.

Floored with sand-covered wood, the arena itself was 83 by 48 meters (272 by 157 ft) and served by 80 shafts that were used to bring animals and victims, to the surface from the warren of tunnels, cells and cages below. A low surrounding wall meant that the arena could be flooded and mock sea battles staged. Indeed, the shows that Romans flocked to see in their tens of thousands were almost always grisly. Wild beasts of every kind, including rhinoceros and elephants, as well as lions, bears and crocodiles were brought here from distant corners of the Empire and beyond to fight professional gladiators and terrified criminals or Christians.

To commemorate a military victory in 107 AD, the Emperor Trajan is reported to have ordered 123 days of slaughter, involving 10,000 gladiators and 11,000 animals.

Today, the Colosseum is partly ruined. It fell into disuse around the 6th century. Much of its stone was taken for other building projects in medieval times and it was rocked by an earthquake in 1349. Nevertheless, its magnificent broken walls and exposed maze of tunnels and cells remain an excellent illustration of Rome's architectural and engineering genius as well as the cruelty of its civilization.

Main image: *A view of the interior of the Colosseum, showing the subterranean area where caged animals would have been held in readiness.*

Inset: *Now mostly ruined, in the 1st century AD the façade of the Colosseum was faced with travertine and featured 80 entrances, including private doors for the emperor and the Vestal Virgins.*

DEATH VALLEY

Death Valley is the hottest place in the Western Hemisphere, with a record temperature of 56.7°C (134°F) being recorded on July 13, 1913. Despite this, it is far from being the flat, sweltering and lifeless place of popular misconception. In fact, Death Valley is an area rich in incredible scenic beauty; a desert of shifting sand dunes, jagged canyons and banded rock, overlooked by snow-capped peaks. The valley contains a surprising variety of flora and fauna and is of huge geological interest. It also occupies an almost mythical place in American culture.

It is located in the Mojave Desert, on the border of California and Nevada. At 86 meters (282 ft) below sea level, its Badwater Basin salt pan is the lowest point in North America, and lies just 123 kilometers (76 miles) from Mount Whitney, which is the highest point in the 48 contiguous states of the mainland US. On a clear day it is possible to see both from the same viewing point. Now part of the larger Death Valley National Park, the valley itself is a narrow strip some 210 kilometers (130 miles) long and between 10–21 kilometers (6–13 miles) wide, bounded on either side by the Amargosa and Panamint ranges that – along with other ranges that lie between the valley and the ocean – trap precipitation. In fact, the valley has the lowest annual rainfall on the continent and has gone as long as 40 months, since records began, without a single drop.

The desert does, however, receive run off meltwater from the surrounding mountains – often in the form of rushing floods – and harbors springs that nurture a large number of species of plants and animals. Desert bighorn sheep are the best known of the native species, but a variety of other mammals, reptiles and birds also thrive here. Even desert fish have made their home in the waters of Salt Creek. For some 1,000 years the area was also home to the Native-American Timbisha tribe, who called it Tümpisa (meaning 'rock paint') for the paint they made from the valley's clay. It earned its English name during the Gold Rush in 1848, when prospectors had to cross it to reach the gold fields. Although it is reported that the desert claimed only a single life during the Gold Rush period, the name stuck.

Such are the natural wonders of the valley that, after being a center of silver and borax mining from the late 19th century, it was placed under Federal protection in 1933 and designated Death Valley National Monument by President Hoover. In 1994, it became a National Park. Since then, the California Desert Protection Act has added several neighboring valleys to the overall area of the park, though Death Valley remains the most celebrated and beautiful.

Main image: *The fierce sun, thin plant cover and clear air means that the desert surface of Death Valley becomes extremely hot. As the heat radiates through the night, temperatures may drop only a few degrees.*

Inset: *The arid plains of Badwater Basin are the lowest point in North America at 86 meters (282 ft) below sea level.*

DELPHI

The spiritual center of the Ancient Greek world, Delphi was believed to be the dwelling place of the Delphic Oracle through whom the god Apollo – son of Zeus – spoke. It is unsurprising that the ancients thought the place blessed, for in a country that is abounding in natural beauty it is a truly outstanding site. Built on the slopes of Mount Parnassus, the ancient temples, monuments, statues and theater command sweeping vistas over the cypress and olive trees of the Pleistos Valley to the glittering blue waters of the Corinthian Gulf in the distance.

Located in lower central Greece, Delphi is steeped in myth and boasts some of the most important relics of Ancient Greece. The Greeks believed Delphi to be the 'navel of the world,' the place where the earthly and heavenly planes touched. Legend has it that Zeus released two eagles from the ends of the Earth and declared Delphi, the place where they met, the center. A carved stone, known as the 'omphalos,' marked the exact spot. As such, it was a deeply holy – and magical – site. The most famous of the ruins found here is the sanctuary of Apollo within which the priestess of the oracle, known as the Pythia, once sat

on a tripod over a crevasse. Wreathed in vapors rising from deep within the earth she would enter a trance, answering the questions of supplicants and prophesying the future. Among those who visited the oracle was Philip II of Macedonia, the father of Alexander the Great, who is said to have heard of his own impending murder from the Pythia's lips. The ruins that stand on the site today are the remains of a temple that was built in the 4th century BC to replace a previous structure (dating to the 6th century BC) that was destroyed by fire.

While the sanctuary of Apollo is undoubtedly the most renowned of Delphi's archeological wonders there are many others close by. Perhaps the most picturesque is the Tholos at the sanctuary of Athena. The small, columned, circular building dates to around 370 BC and has been partially restored. Delphi was also famous as the site of the Pythian Games, which – like the Olympic Games, of which they were a forerunner – were held every four years. Reminding modern visitors of Delphi's athletic heritage are the remains of the ancient stadium and numerous statues of athletes, including the superb *Charioteer of Delphi*. The Greeks also had a great passion for the stage

and Delphi boasts one of the most spectacular theaters in the world. Built higher up the mountain from the Temple of Apollo, the audience could look down on the stage with the sanctuary complex and the valley beyond as a backdrop.

Now a UNESCO World Heritage Site, Delphi's striking beauty and atmospheric ruins give modern visitors a unique glimpse of Greece's mythic past.

Main image: *The Tholos at Delphi, built between 380 and 360 BC, was originally a circular building enclosed by 20 Doric columns. Only three now remain.*

Inset: *After an earthquake in 373 BC, much of the Temple of Apollo at Delphi was destroyed. These columns are all that remain of the original structure.*

EASTER ISLAND

The most isolated, inhabited spot on Earth, Easter Island – or Rapa Nui as it was named by its native inhabitants – is also one of the most mysterious. Most famous for its 887 huge *moai* (the great stylized statues that dot its landscape), the island was once the home of a thriving civilization – a civilization that had almost vanished by the time it was discovered by European explorers.

Easter Island is the peak of a great volcano that rises from the Pacific seabed 3,510 kilometers (2,180 miles) west of the coast of Chile. At just 24.6 kilometers (15.5 miles) long and measuring 12.3 kilometers (7.6 miles) at its widest point, it is a small island of crater lakes, ancient lava formations and beaches hemmed by the clear blue ocean. Yet, despite its size, archeologists believe that at the peak of its civilization Rapa Nui supported a population of up to 10,000 souls. In isolation, these people developed a complex culture with a distinct and sophisticated writing system and a religion centered on the great *moai* statues that were believed to act as containers for sacred spirits.

Nevertheless, by the time the Dutch navigator Jacob Roggeveen became the first European to set foot on the island on Easter Sunday (April 5) 1722, there were only about 2,000 native people left. Later reports from sailors such as the celebrated British explorer, James Cook (who arrived in 1774) suggested that the island seemed largely barren and the *moai* monuments were toppled and neglected. Over the next century, the remaining islanders were further decimated by slavery, the introduction of European diseases and forced deportation.

The questions of where the island's original inhabitants came from and what happened to their once prosperous culture have been the source of many conflicting theories. Some have suggested that Easter Island was the highest of a populated chain of islands that was submerged when ocean levels rose at the end of the last ice age, but this has been widely discounted. It is more likely that the first Easter Islanders were a small group of Polynesians who were washed up here after being lost at sea. Finding an island rich in plant, animal and birdlife, and surrounded by waters abundant in fish, their numbers increased and – like other cultures in similar happy circumstances – devoted their time to creative arts and religion. However, at some point, the population

became too large for the island to sustain and, having stripped it of its resources, the islanders' society collapsed. The famine may even have paved the way to cannibalism.

What remains of this civilization is one of the most distinctive and eerily beautiful landscapes in the world. The solemn faces of Easter Island's *moai*, some of which are up to 10 meters (33 ft) tall, dominate the island. The statues create an unbroken chain around the circumference, and more are dotted throughout the interior. Many have now been restored to their original erect positions and stand as a memorial to a once great civilization.

Main image: *The crater lake, Rano Kau, is one of the only sources of fresh water on Easter Island as there are no other permanent streams or rivers.*

Inset: *These eerie stone sculptures, or* moai, *are often referred to as 'Easter Island heads.' However, most of the statues were carved as kneeling figures but shifting earth has buried their lower parts.*

EIFFEL TOWER

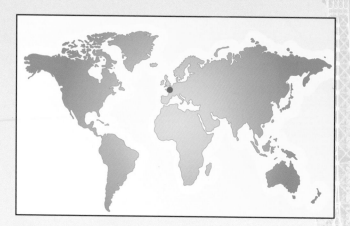

Towering above Paris, the Eiffel Tower is an international icon and one of the best known structures in the world. A simple design built of iron, it nevertheless lends its home city a unique elegance and has become a treasured symbol of the French capital since it was built in the late 19th century.

For over 40 years the world's tallest building (until the completion of New York's Chrysler Building), the Eiffel Tower rises to a height of 324 meters (1,063 ft), growing taller by up to 18 centimeters (7 in) depending on the temperature. It stands on the Champ de Mars, Paris's old military training grounds, and was designed by architect, Gustave Eiffel to provide a grand entrance to the 1889 Exposition Universelle World's Fair. In planning the tower, Eiffel gave great thought to the structure's ability to withstand high winds, and its gently curving, four-sided shape was based as much on mathematical calculations of wind resistance as aesthetic considerations.

Construction took two years, two months and five days between 1887 and 1889, during which 100 ironworkers produced the 18,038 pieces of its lattice frame while 121 men worked on site to join the parts, using 2.5 million rivets. During the building work, Eiffel took a firm hand in safety regulations, which were unusually strict for the times, and thanks to the methods he devised to ensure the workers' safety only one man died during construction. When completed, it was coated with 36 tonnes (40 tons) of paint to prevent it rusting (a process that is now repeated every seven years and takes 18 months). Despite its tremendous size, the finished tower is relatively lightweight at a modest 9,072 tonnes (10,000 tons) and it sways just 5 centimeters (2 in) or so in high winds.

Although it is now a much loved component of the Paris skyline, at the time of its completion many prominent Parisians hated the new tower. One critic, the novelist Guy de Maupassant, climbed to its restaurant each day, explaining that it was the only place in the city from where he couldn't see the Eiffel Tower. Many others wrote angry letters of complaint to newspapers and journals. Nevertheless, Parisian affection for the structure grew and it also proved so useful for communications (it was fitted with broadcast antennas) that when the time came for it to be taken down, the authorities decided to let it stay instead. Over the century or so since then, the Eiffel Tower has become an integral part of the city and a feature recognized by billions around the world.

Since it was officially opened on May 6, 1889, over 200 million people have visited the Eiffel Tower, and millions more continue to do so each year, making it not only France's most popular attraction, but among the most visited structures in the world.

Opposite page: *The Eiffel Tower, perhaps the most identifiable monument in the world, was completed in 1889 and originally acted as a gateway to the Parisian World's Fair.*

Left: *The Eiffel Tower was never meant to be a permanent fixture on the Paris skyline. The initial permit was for only 20 years, after which it was supposed to have been dismantled.*

EL DJEM AMPHITHEATER

Dominating the skyline of the otherwise unremarkable Tunisian town of El Djem is one of the finest relics of the Roman age, an amphitheater only slightly smaller than Rome's famous Colosseum and in a much better state of preservation. Walking through its cells and holding pens, seating areas and colonnades, it is still easy to imagine the imposing building thronged with thousands of spectators cheering on the gladiators, the sweat and tension in the galleries beneath the arena and the howls and roars of caged wild beasts.

Located about 210 kilometers (130 miles) south of the city of Tunis, the town of El Djem was founded by the Romans in 46 BC and named Thysdrus. Although it was not destined to become the greatest of cities, the locally produced olive oil was widely held to be the best in the empire and, over time, it became a bustling, wealthy port and trading hub. With profit came ever more ambitious building works, of which the amphitheater was the greatest, and probably the last.

Building began early in the 3rd century AD and, when finished, the amphitheater was 148 meters (485 ft) long and 122 meters (400 ft) wide. Constructed of red limestone quarried from Salakta, 30 kilometers (18 miles) away, the three tiers of its seating areas rise to 35 meters (115 ft) with the highest tier featuring shaded 'rooms' for the most important and wealthy guests. It is estimated that at full capacity it could have held around 35,000 spectators, or roughly the entire permanent population of the town at that time (much of the audience would have been made up of visiting dignitaries, soldiers, sailors and merchants). The arena itself is 65 meters (213 ft) by 39 meters (128 ft), and beneath are two basement galleries where the gladiators and various animals would have been kept. It is still possible to see the holes in the arena floor through which the beasts would have been raised to do combat.

Some archeologists believe that the amphitheater was never completely finished. Under the rule of a proconsul (governor) called Gordian, the town became involved in a revolt against Rome in 238 AD, probably instigated by a new tax on olive oil. Gordian was proclaimed 'emperor' but his rule was short-lived. Within weeks he was dead and Thysdrus declined quickly. Nevertheless, its magnificent amphitheater has survived the following centuries remarkably well. Despite being plundered of its stone for various building projects and coming under attack during World War II when German soldiers used it as a refuge, it is amazingly intact and remains a magnificent example of Imperial Roman architecture.

Main image: *The Roman amphitheater of El Djem could seat an audience of 35,000 and was built around 238 AD.*

Inset: *El Djem withstood the ravages of time until the 17th century, when many of its stones were taken to Kairouan, during construction of the Great Mosque.*

EMPIRE STATE BUILDING

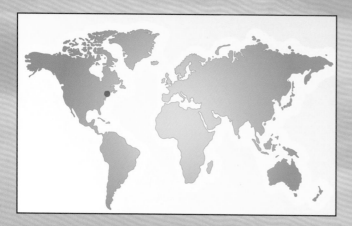

A masterpiece of Art Deco design and one of the world's most iconic buildings, New York City's Empire State Building was chosen by the American Society of Civil Engineers as one of its Seven Wonders of the Modern World in 1994. In compiling the list, the ASCE paid tribute to 'modern society's ability to achieve the unachievable, reach unreachable heights, and scorn the notion of "it can't be done."' All this and more can be said of the Empire State. While it is no longer the tallest building in the world, it remains one of the most instantly recognizable and, as the ASCE point out, the standard against which all others are judged.

Located on Fifth Avenue at West 34th Street in New York City, the Empire State Building is 381 meters (1,250 ft) in height at the 102nd floor roof, with its spire adding a little over 62 meters (203 ft) to its overall stature. It was designed by William F. Lamb of the Shreve, Lamb and Harmon architectural company and was a groundbreaking structure in numerous ways. Not only was the Empire State the tallest building in the world for over 40 years (from its completion in 1931 until the North Tower of the World Trade Center was finished in 1972), but it was also the first building in the world of over 100 floors and had an unprecedented 64 elevators (now 73). Its construction, too, was remarkable. Lamb produced his designs in just two weeks and, from start to finish, the entire building took just 410 days to complete, averaging 4.5 floors each week; faster than any skyscraper had ever been constructed before. Over 3,400 workers swarmed over the building as it rose, and photographs of them nonchalantly eating lunch while sitting on girders hundreds of feet above the city are now a part of the Empire State Building's – and the city's – great heritage.

Officially opened on May 1, 1931, the finished Empire State is a superb example of Art Deco

symmetry and was an immediate hit with New Yorkers and tourists who eagerly paid the two dollar fee to view the city from its observation decks. However, its doors opened during the Great Depression and it took some years to fill the building's 200,500 square meters (2,158,000 sq ft) of office space, a fact that led New Yorkers to give it the nickname 'Empty State Building' for some time after it opened.

Since then, the Empire State Building has become America's favorite work of architecture – according to the American Institute of Architects – a symbol of New York throughout the world and the star of many movies. In 1964, floodlights were installed at the top of the building and the higher stories of the Empire State now glow at night with patriotic or seasonal colors.

Main image: *The Empire State Building in New York was the tallest building in the world on its completion in 1931 and held that record for over 40 years.*

Inset: *The famous Art Deco spire was designed as a mooring mast for airships. The idea was abandoned after the first few attempts proved too dangerous.*

Following pages: *Lit in red, white and blue to commemorate the September 11 terrorist attacks, the Empire State Building still dominates the Manhattan skyline.*

MOUNT EVEREST

On the border of Nepal and Tibet is the tallest: Mount Everest. As the process that formed the range continues, Everest still rises by 4 millimeters (0.157 in) a year.

The name by which it is now commonly known was given to the peak in honor of Colonel Sir George Everest, the British Surveyor General of India between 1830 and 1843. Known as Peak 15 to the British survey team who first attempted to gauge its height, it was not until 1847 that James Nicholson, under the orders of Andrew Waugh, made scientific measurements of the mountain. Using his theodolite from several points over 160 kilometers (100 miles) away, Nicholson established its height at 9,200 meters (30,200 ft) though this was later verified and amended. It was not until 1856 that a much more accurate figure of 8,840 meters (29,002 ft) was publicly announced. (Interestingly, the height was thought to be exactly 29,000 ft but an extra 2 ft were added to make it seem as if the number had not been rounded up or down.) The survey team's policy was to keep native names wherever possible, but as neither Nepal nor Tibet would allow them to cross their borders they were unable to establish for certain what it was called by the local people. Instead, Waugh chose to name it after his predecessor, against Everest's wishes, and the name was adopted by the Royal Geographical Society.

Known as Qomolangma Peak (meaning 'mother goddess of the earth') in Tibet and Mount Sagarmatha ('goddess of the sky') in Nepal, the Earth's crowning peak rises from the Himalayas to a height of 8,848 meters (29,029 ft) above sea level. A sacred mountain to Buddhists, and the site of two important monasteries, its majestic summit has beckoned thousands of climbers from around the globe over the years.

The Himalayan mountain range was born about 50 million years ago when the landmass now known as India crashed into the Eurasian continent at a speed of about 10 centimeters (4 in) per year. As the subcontinent continued to plough upward, over millions of years the land buckled into vast folds that were pushed ever higher by gigantic pressures from beneath the Earth's crust. These primal forces created a range that now contains over 100 of the world's highest peaks.

The privilege of conquering the highest mountain in the world has drawn many to Everest over the years. Several unsuccessful attempts were made in the 1920s, which cost numerous lives including those of native porters and mountaineers, George Mallory and Andrew Irvine. A successful attempt on the summit was made in 1953, with Sir Edmund Hillary and Tenzing Norgay being the first confirmed mountaineers to reach the peak on May 29 of that year. Since then over 4,000 men and women have ascended Everest's mighty flanks, ranging from the 13-year-old boy, Jordan Romero, to Min Bahadur Sherchan, who reached the peak in 2008 aged 76.

Opposite page: *The highest mountain on the planet at 8,848 meters (29,029 ft), Mount Everest was first scaled by Edmund Hillary and Tenzing Norgay in 1953.*

Inset: *The stunning view from the peak of Mount Everest. The mountain has now been climbed over 4,000 times, though it remains a dangerous challenge and the bodies of 150 mountaineers remain lost on its flanks.*

EVERGLADES

Everglades National Park. Home to nine different ecosystems, including sawgrass prairie, mangrove forests, cypress swamps and rocky outcrops strewn with pines, the area supports a great profusion of flora and fauna, much of which is unique to the area. A region of rare natural beauty that is also integral to southern Florida's environmental wellbeing, the Everglades have suffered from a lack of human understanding of their importance over the past century, but great efforts are now being made to reverse the damage inflicted during that time.

The Everglades system begins to the north of Florida with the Kissimmee River, which flows southward to Lake Okeechobee, the United States' second-largest freshwater lake. In the wet season, the vast, shallow lake becomes the source of a sheet of water that flows slowly south, creating a great watershed that is prone to flooding in the wet season and drought and fire in the dry. Characterized by sawgrass marshes interspersed with deeper ponds and channels, and dotted with dense stands of

Occupying a large section of southern Florida, the Everglades constitute the biggest subtropical wetland wilderness in the United States, with a fifth of their total area protected as

trees, the Everglades have evolved distinctive, interdependent habitats. And where swamp meets the ocean, the Everglades change again, becoming an estuarine mangrove system of forested shore and islands.

These diverse habitats sustain a host of different species ranging from alligators, crocodiles, snakes and other reptiles to bobcats and deer, as well as 260 species of bird. Among the area's wildlife are 15 endangered species, including sea turtles and West Indian Manatees. For thousands of years the Everglades were also the home of the Calusa Indians, who ranged over long distances by canoe. Tragically, these highly civilized people were decimated by the introduction of European diseases after the arrival of the Spanish in 1513.

European colonists later wreaked further havoc on the delicate Everglade ecosystems by draining large swathes of what they saw as useless swamp to make way for farmland and urban areas. Unchecked hunting took a toll on the area's wildlife, while the addition of chemical fertilizers to the swamp soil in the 1920s began to change the Everglades' plant life. The construction of the Hoover Dike on Lake Okeechobee in the 1930s disrupted the natural flow of the region's seasonal rhythms.

Fortunately, it was realized that the Everglades were in danger of being completely destroyed and, in 1947, the United States government created Everglades National Park in order to protect a large area of the region from further damage. Since then, UNESCO has adopted the area as a World Heritage Site and, on December 11, 2000, President Bill Clinton signed the Comprehensive Everglades Restoration Plan, beginning the world's biggest program of environmental repair.

Today, over a million visitors each year enjoy the natural wonders of the Everglades National Park. With the State of Florida spending tens of millions of dollars annually in protection and restoration, the future of this exceptional wilderness is looking brighter than it has done for many years.

Main image: *The sawgrass marshes of the Everglades covered a third of the Florida Peninsula before drainage began in 1905.*

Inset: *Dividing the sawgrass marshes are 'sloughs' – areas of free flowing water that are a habitat for alligators, turtles, snakes and fish.*

FORBIDDEN CITY

As befitted an emperor who was believed by his subjects to be the son of Heaven, Beijing's Forbidden City is a magnificent palace complex, representing the peak of Chinese architectural achievement. Built to recreate paradise on Earth, entrance was strictly prohibited to the ordinary people of China – hence its name – and it served as the imperial family's residence and the hub of Chinese government for almost 500 years. Steeped in a rich heritage, and providing an unparalleled record of the opulence of China's imperial past, the Forbidden City is the largest palace complex in the world and is listed by UNESCO as one of the five most important.

On the instruction of Zhu Di, the third emperor of the Ming Dynasty, work on the complex began in 1406 AD and continued for 15 years. During that time up to a million artisans and laborers worked ceaselessly to create a citadel of dizzying splendor from rare wood, marble and the prized 'golden' bricks made in Suzhou. When complete, the 'city' was a rectangular complex of 72 hectares (178 acres) surrounded by 7.9-meter (26-ft) high walls measuring 961 meters (3,153 ft) from north to south and 753 meters (2,470 ft) from east to west. Containing hundreds of buildings (980 still exist), and small but beautifully landscaped gardens, it was split into two sections. The southern (called the Outer Court) was reserved for ceremonial use and the northern (Inner Court) contained the palaces of the emperor and empress as well as quarters for other members of the royal family, courtiers and retainers as well as administrative buildings.

At the center is the Hall of Supreme Harmony. The most well-known of the complex's structures, and the largest, this was the very heart of the Chinese Empire. It was built on

three levels of marble and surrounded by incense burners, and beneath the double-layered roof, which was a design used solely for imperial buildings, the emperor conducted business of state from the Dragon Throne. It was also the venue for imperial marriages and enthronements. Elsewhere is the Palace of Heavenly Purity, the emperor's personal palace, the Palace of Heavenly Tranquility, where the empress lived, and many other halls. Most of the buildings are roofed with yellow tiles (yellow was the color of the emperor) and are adorned with symbolic details, such as the dragons that line each roof. At its peak the complex was a gigantic trove of exquisite paintings, ceramics, sculptures and other treasures.

Puyi, the last Emperor of China, abdicated in 1912, but continued living in the Inner Court until 1924 when he was ousted. The complex was damaged slightly during the civil war which led to the establishment of the People's Republic of China, but came under the personal protection of premier Zhou Enlai during the Cultural Revolution of 1966–1976, which saved the buildings from almost certain destruction. Now a vast museum, displaying many of the riches of the Chinese emperors, the Forbidden City is one of China's most visited sites.

Main image: *The Hall of Supreme Harmony is the largest surviving wooden structure, not only inside the Forbidden City but in the whole of China.*

Inset: *The palace boasts almost 10,000 bronze pieces, many dating as far back as the Shang Dynasty, which was established in 1766 BC.*

FORUM OF ROME

The Roman Empire was one of the most powerful the world has ever seen. Stretching across Europe, the Middle East and North Africa, its influence lasted centuries and its legacies are still entwined in the culture of the modern Western world. At the center of that mighty domain was the city itself, and at the heart of Rome was the Forum; the hub of political, judicial, religious and social life. Here, the empire's powerful people met to debate the latest conquests, nobles addressed the people and Rome came to celebrate.

The area was originally marshland between the Capitoline Hill and the Palatine Hill, but was drained by the Cloaca Maxima sewer, which was constructed almost 3,000 years ago and is still in use today. Based on the Ancient Greek example of a town square, the area became a busy market and meeting place. Over the years the Forum acquired important buildings such as the Temple of Vesta and home of the Vestal Virgins as well as the royal palace, or Regia, both built during the reign of Numa Pompilius (753–673 BC), Rome's second king.

The Forum continued to expand and grow in importance after Rome overthrew its monarchy (around 509 BC) and became a republic. Private houses were demolished, the area paved and grand temples were built such as the Temple of Castor and Pollux (which also served as a meeting place for the Senate), Temple of Saturn and the Temple of Concord.

As Rome's power grew, so the Forum gained more monumental buildings. Beginning in 54 BC, Julius Caesar expanded the northeast section, making new areas for state business as well as replacing the Curia with a new building and raising a shrine to himself. Later additions included triumphal arches such as the Arch of Septimius Severus, which was completed in 203 AD to commemorate Caesar's victories over the Parthians.

After the Western Roman Empire fell in the 5th century AD, the city's power waned and, over the centuries, the Forum fell into disrepair. Silt from the flooding River Tiber covered its paving and its superb Classical buildings were plundered for their stone. By Medieval times it was being used as a cattle pasture. However, as academic interest in the Roman period grew, 19th century archeologists began excavating the site, a process that was finished early in the 20th century. The Forum is now one of Rome's most visited sites and, though mostly ruined, it is still easy to imagine the scale and grandeur of the city at its imperial peak while walking among its remains.

Opposite page: *The ruins of the Forum at dusk with the Colosseum visible in the distance.*

Left: *The towering ruins of the Temple of Saturn (left) and the Temple of Vespasian (right) dominate the western end of the Roman Forum.*

MOUNT FUJI

The most holy of Japan's three holy mountains and, at 3,776 meters (12,388 ft), the highest in the country, Mount Fuji is a spellbinding part of the Japanese landscape that has inspired artists and poets throughout history. Today, its famously symmetrical, cone-shaped peak, skirted by lakes, cherry trees and forest, attracts tens of thousands of pilgrims and tourists each year.

Classified as an active volcano with a low eruption risk, Mount Fuji – or Fujiyama as it is sometimes known – is west of the Japanese capital, Tokyo. It lies at the conjunction of three tectonic plates and was formed over successive major eruptions, the last of which occurred about 10,000 years ago. Less dramatic eruptions have happened since then, however – the last was between December 1707 and January 1708 and gave the mountain a new crater 487 meters (1,600 ft) in diameter as well as a new peak midway up its slope. There has been no sign of activity since. A part of the Fuji-Hakone-Izu National Park, it is surrounded by five lakes (Lake Kawaguchi, Lake Yamanaka, Lake Sai, Lake Motosu and Lake Shoji) and the Aokigahara forest, which is said to be haunted by ghosts and demons, also lies at its base.

Ancient remains suggest that Fuji has been a holy place for almost as long as humans have lived in Japan. The Ainu people, who were the country's aboriginal inhabitants, held it sacred, while Shintoists and Buddhists also designated it as a holy place. Today, climbing its shrine-strewn slopes remains an important pilgrimage for many Japanese, though they are likely to be joined on the arduous trek by a large number of

tourists also making the eight-hour walk to the peak. Although climbers are dissuaded from making the ascent for most of the year because of the snow and freezing temperatures, in July and August much of the snow melts and tens of thousands make the trip up Fuji's slopes. Various paths are dotted with rest stops, shrines and antique teahouses that help make the climb a quintessentially Japanese experience. Many choose to ascend at night in order to see the sunrise from the peak.

Although it is uncertain how the name 'Fuji' originated, the mountain's nickname is *Konohanasakua-hime*, which translates as 'causing the blossom to bloom brightly.' Undoubtedly the best time to see Mount Fuji – if not climb it – is in the spring when its snowy peak rises above the cherry blossom.

Main image: *Measuring 3,776 meters (12,388 ft), the tranquil exterior of Mount Fuji belies the fact it is still classed as an active volcano, although its last eruption was over 300 years ago.*

Inset: *An aerial view of the snow capped summit of Mount Fuji.*

GALAPAGOS ISLANDS

Formed two or three million years ago by volcanic activity, in geological terms the Galapagos Islands are young, but in their relatively short history, the 18 isolated islands have evolved an incredible variety of unique flora and fauna. Famous for the giant tortoises found there, the islands are most celebrated for helping prompt Charles Darwin to develop the theory of evolution. In 1835, the naturalist wrote in his journal, during his visit, 'The natural history of this archipelago is very remarkable: it seems to be a little world within itself.'

The islands lie on the Equator, 973 kilometers (605 miles) off the coast of Ecuador, to which country they belong. In fact, the Equator roughly bisects the chain with some islands situated in the northern hemisphere, and some in the southern. The archipelago is comprised of 15 main islands – the largest being Isabela Island which, at 4,640 square kilometers (1,790 sq miles), is four times the size of the second largest – three smaller islands and 107 tiny islets and rocks. Situated on the meeting place of three tectonic plates and over a volcanic phenomenon known as the Galapagos Hotspot, the islands are still in the process of formation. In 2009, for example, an eruption on Fernandina sent lava flowing into the ocean, adding new coastline to the island.

The islands' isolation, their volcanic nature, and the fact that they are relatively arid, created a unique environment for the species that found their way here. A lack of natural predators enabled them to flourish, but scarcity of food encouraged swift adaptation to the new environment. A good example is the Darwin finch, of which there are 13 species all descended from a common ancestor species. It was study of these finches, when he had returned to England, that led Darwin to the theory of natural selection and evolution.

The first Europeans to set foot on the islands were Spanish, a party on their way to Peru under the command of the Bishop of Panama, Fray Tomás de Berlanga, who were blown off course and landed in 1535. The islands soon became known as the Insulae de los Galopegos (Islands of the Tortoises) for their most prominent inhabitants. They were later used as a refuge by English pirates, then, in the 19th century, as a base for whalers. Excessive hunting devastated the island's wildlife during that period, with some species being lost forever, but in the 1930s Ecuador passed legislation to make the islands a national park. In 1978, UNESCO adopted them as a World Heritage Site then, in 1985, as a Biosphere Reserve. Today, the islands have a population of around 40,000 people, many of whom service a busy tourist industry. Almost the entire surface area of the islands, along with 70,000 square kilometers (27,000 sq miles) of the surrounding ocean, are fiercely protected.

Main image: *The unique landscape of Isabela Island was formed by the merging of six volcanoes.*

Inset: *A giant Galapagos tortoise on the rim of Alcedo Volcano on Isabela Island. The population of tortoises on Alcedo Volcano is the largest group in the archipegalo.*

GIANT'S CAUSEWAY

Every so often, nature conspires to produce a landscape so unusual that it is difficult to believe it was created without human intervention. Such a phenomenon is the Giant's Causeway. With its 40,000 symmetrical, mostly hexagonal, basalt columns interlocking perfectly and rising above the sea on the rugged, northeast Irish coast, the causeway is a breathtaking sight, and a wonder that seems to have been created by supernatural beings for some mythical purpose. It is hardly surprising then, that the Giant's Causeway is steeped in legend.

Located in the county of Antrim Northern Ireland, 3 kilometers (2 miles) from the town of Bushmills, the Giant's Causeway was, in fact, created by wholly naturally forces. Roughly 60 million years ago, molten basalt lava erupted from beneath the ground and formed a sheet over the area's chalk bed. On contact with water, the rock cooled rapidly, contracted and fractured into the distinctive crystallized hexagonal pattern that forms 'stepping stones' up to 12 meters (36 ft) high that lead out from the base of the local cliffs into the Atlantic. Although the Giant's Causeway is the most famous, and most scenic, example of the phenomenon, comparable formations can be found scattered around the globe. The same lava flow,

in fact, created similar columns at Fingal's Cave in the island of Staffa, Scotland.

While the geological forces that formed the Giant's Causeway are no mystery now, to Ireland's ancient people, the stones must have been an astonishing, perplexing spectacle and a number of legends arose to explain their creation. The most popular of these was the tale of Fionn mac Cumhaill, (Finn McCool) who is said to have made the causeway so that he could walk across to Scotland to challenge Benandonner, the giant of Scotland. There are several versions of the story, but each has a similar theme: Fionn is surprised by his counterpart's size and a plot is hatched between Fionn and his wife, Oonagh, to trick him. When Benandonner crosses the causeway he finds Ooonagh with a sleeping baby – Fionn, covered in blankets. Oonagh tells the Scottish giant that he will have to wait for Fionn to return, but Benandonner, seeing the size of the baby is struck with terror, imagining that the father

of such a child must be huge indeed. Benandonner runs back to Scotland for his life, tearing up the causeway as he flees.

Today, the Giant's Causeway is one of the United Kingdom's best loved natural wonders, a National Nature Reserve and a UNESCO World Heritage Site. It has been popular with tourists since the 19th century and protected by the British National Trust since the 1960s. Since then, much effort has been made to keep the site as pristine as it would have appeared to Ireland's first inhabitants.

Main image: *Another of the legends surrounding the Giant's Causeway describes how Fionn mac Cumhaill, or Finn McCool, built it trying to reach his lover across the sea in Scotland.*

Inset: *The basalt columns of the Giant's Causeway were formed over 60 million years ago.*

GOLDEN GATE BRIDGE

Numerous cities, such as Paris, London and New York, have become inextricably associated with their most striking buildings. The structure that millions of people around the world identify with the city of San Francisco is the Golden Gate Bridge. A groundbreaking span of simple elegance, it was once the longest suspension bridge in the world and – when finished – perfectly captured the Californian spirit of pioneering know-how.

The Golden Gate Bridge spans the mouth of San Francisco Bay, where it meets the Pacific Ocean, connecting the city to Marin County. It was built between 1933 and 1937, after years of discussion during which many engineers and architects argued that it would be impossible to bridge the strait. Indeed, the project presented many difficulties. The strait plunges to a depth of 152 meters (500 ft) in the middle of the channel, and also has strong tides. Fierce winds are not uncommon and the area is also frequently swathed in the thick fog for which the city is so famous. It was also thought that the cost of any bridge that could successfully span the 2,042-meter (6,700-ft) strait would be ruinously high.

Nevertheless, in 1916, an article appeared in the *San Francisco Bulletin*, calling for engineers to address the problem. In reply, Joseph Strauss designed a bridge that he calculated could be built for just $17 million (San Francisco's city engineer had anticipated the cost would be closer to $100 million). For over a decade Strauss's plans were refined in collaboration with other engineers and architects and work finally began on January 5, 1933. Strauss was named head of the project, though because he had previously only built drawbridges and was unfamiliar with the technologies involved in cable-suspension, much of the design work fell to architect Irving Morrow and the senior engineer Charles Alton Ellis. In fact, though Strauss tried to secure his place in posterity by downplaying the input of others (even sacking Ellis in 1931, though he continued to work on, unpaid), Ellis was recognized as the Golden Gate's major designer in 2007. However, Strauss worked tirelessly on the project and contributed many ideas. He was also responsible for developing safety devices such as movable netting, which saved 19 lives, though in all 11 were lost during construction.

The finished bridge cost just over $35 million and was painted with a vibrant red-orange. It was officially opened on May 27, 1937, with celebrations lasting a week and some 200,000 people crossing it by foot and roller skate before it was opened to traffic. Although it is no longer the world's longest bridge, it is still the second longest suspension main span in the United States (after the Varrazano-Narrows Bridge) and is a popular tourist attraction as well as being placed fifth on the American Institute of Architects' List of America's Favorite Architecture.

Main image: *The Golden Gate Bridge from Marin County, looking toward the sprawling city of San Francisco.*

Inset: *The iconic towers of the Golden Gate Bridge measure 230 meters (754 ft). At the time of its completion, it was the tallest suspension bridge in the world as well as the longest.*

GRAND CANYON

Etched into the Arizona landscape by the Colorado River over millions of years, the Grand Canyon is one of nature's most awe-inspiring spectacles. Many have tried to communicate its wonders, and though it is impossible to capture the canyon's splendor with words, the American explorer John Wesley Powell perhaps came close when he wrote, 'The glories and the beauties of form, color, and sound unite in the Grand Canyon – forms unrivaled even by the mountains, colors that vie with sunsets, and sounds that span the diapason from tempest to tinkling raindrop, from cataract [waterfall] to bubbling fountain.'

Although statistics alone cannot do justice to the canyon's breathtaking beauty, they can give some idea of its scale and features. It stretches over 445 kilometers (277 miles) from Lee's Ferry on the Arizona/Utah border to Grand Wash Cliffs, close to Las Vegas. The north and south rims are, in places, only about 400 meters (1,300 ft) apart while in others the chasm widens to a 29 kilometers (18 miles). In some areas, the canyon is over 1.6 kilometers (1 mile) deep from rim to the Colorado River which winds through its floor, and the steep, water-eroded cliffs are banded with layers of rock formed over two billion years.

Archeologists believe that the canyon has been inhabited by human beings for almost 12,000 years. Many Native American peoples have lived here over that time and left relics of their passing, including granaries carved into the cliff walls. The first European to visit was the Spanish conquistador Garcia López de Cárdenas, who arrived in 1540, though the canyon remained unexplored until the late 18th century when Spanish soldiers attempted to find a way to cross it. Later visitors included trappers and Mormon missionaries also seeking a way across. The canyon first came under US federal protection in 1908, during the presidency of Theodore Roosevelt. A champion of America's great wildernesses, Roosevelt designated the Grand Canyon as one of the 18 National Monuments created during his term. In 1919, just three years after the service was created, it was designated a National Park and the total protected area has been extended several times since.

Home to a bewildering array of flora and fauna, including – most famously – the Californian Condor and rattlesnake, the Grand Canyon has a unique place in the heritage of the United States and is now a National Park, a UNESCO World Heritage Site and one of the United States' most popular tourist attractions, drawing millions of visitors each year. It has also been included among the Seven Wonders of the Natural World. While other canyons are longer, deeper and wider, the Grand Canyon cannot be matched for majesty, particularly at sunrise and sunset when the light appears to make the reds, yellow and oranges of its cliffs glow.

Main image: *The bands of rock exposed by erosion in the Grand Canyon reveal geological processes stretching back two billion years.*

Inset: *On the north rim of the canyon stands Point Imperial, the highest lookout point on that side of the gorge, standing at 2,683 meters (8,803 ft).*

GREAT BARRIER REEF

A vividly colorful world constructed by, and made up of, billion upon billion of tiny coral polyps, Australia's Great Barrier Reef is one of the Seven Wonders of the Natural World and the greatest reef system on Earth. Teeming with life, the warm, shallow waters of the reef support an incredibly rich ecosystem that is similar in diversity to tropical rainforest.

With a total area of approximately 334,400 square kilometers (133,000 sq miles) the great Barrier Reef stretches along the coast of Queensland, northeast Australia, for 2,600 kilometers (1,600 miles). Roughly mirroring the shape of the coastline, it lies between 15 kilometers (9 miles) and 150 kilometers (90 miles) offshore, is up to 65 kilometers (40 miles) wide in places, and made up of about 3,000 individual coral reefs with over 600 islands. Each of the reefs has been formed over thousands of years by minuscule organisms, known as coral polyps. These tiny creatures live in relatively shallow, sun warmed waters and – over time – the colonies grow to create distinctive fan, antler and brain shapes. The brilliant colors associated with coral are, in fact, created by algae that live on the colony's surface.

In effect, the Great Barrier Reef is a giant living organism and, as such, it is extremely delicate. Nevertheless, there is evidence that coral reefs in the area existed up to 600,000 years ago and that the present reef began to form about 20,000 years ago. Over that time it has developed an intricate and rich ecosystem that nurtures a vast array of life. More than 1,500 species of fish alone live among the corals, many of them, such as the clownfish, parrotfish and angelfish, being beautifully colored to match their environment. Larger fish include numerous species of shark, with the most common being the mostly harmless reef shark – though the infamous Great White can also be found in these waters – while mammals include 30 species of whale, dolphins, porpoises and dugongs. The reef also provides a breeding ground for sea turtles and is home to sea snakes, 4,000 species of mollusks and 215 types of bird.

Many factors, including fishing and pollution as well as natural threats such as the Crown of Thorns starfish which devours coral polyps, have combined to threaten this fragile ecosystem in recent years, though the Australian government has responded with a raft of initiatives designed to protect the reef. Although millions of tourists are still welcomed each year, the reef is now one of the two largest marine-protected areas in the world, and large sections are sternly regulated to minimize human impact.

Main image: *Dotted with lush islands fringed with coral beaches and azure waters, the Great Barrier Reef is widely considered one of nature's most beautiful sights.*

Inset: *Just beneath the water's surface, coral beds create the vibrant colors of the Great Barrier Reef.*

GREAT BLUE HOLE

Named by the celebrated ocean explorer Jacques-Yves Cousteau as one of the world's best dive sites, the Great Blue Hole is both a geological marvel and a supremely beautiful underwater site. From above, it is simply a sudden, and astonishing circle of deep indigo amid clear turquoise water, but below the surface it is a wonderland of stalactites, strange limestone formations and caverns that have never been touched by sunlight.

Found in the center of an atoll called Lighthouse Reef, which is about 100 kilometers (62 miles) off the coast of Belize, the Great Blue Hole is thought to be the largest underwater sinkhole in the world. It was formed at the end of the last ice age when rising waters flooded a limestone cave that had previously been above water. Later, the roof fell in, possibly

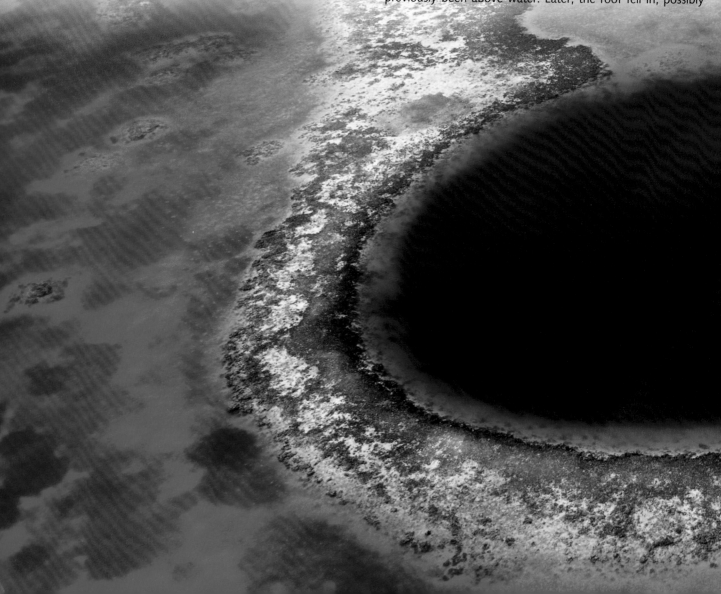

due to an earthquake that also caused the entire cave to tilt about 12 degrees, leaving the cave open at the top.

The hole itself is 300 meters (984 ft) in diameter and surrounded by the shallow, coral filled waters of the atoll. Within the Great Blue Hole, however, the depth plunges to 125 meters (410 ft). For about 44 meters (144 ft), the walls descend almost vertically, but then angle back in overhangs and ledges, from which hang stalactites that become more complex and bizarrely shaped at greater depths. Some are up to 12 meters (40 ft) long with a diameter of 3 meters (10 ft). Closer to the surface swim a vast variety of fish, including giant groupers, nurse sharks, reef sharks and hammerhead sharks, but at deeper levels marine life becomes rarer, due to the still water and lack of sunlight, though divers have reported the occasional sighting of lone sharks. At about 70 meters (230 ft), a narrow tunnel can be found on one wall; it leads to a further series of caves that are also filled with stalactites, but which are completely in darkness. Interestingly, the distant mainland also has a number of sinkholes and it has been suggested that these form part of the same massive cave system.

As a part of the Belize Barrier Reef Reserve System, which includes the close-by Half Moon Caye Natural Monument, the Great Blue Hole has been a protected UNESCO World Heritage Site since 1997. Its crystal waters, abundant life and breathtaking underwater scenery attract thousands of divers each year.

Main image: *From above, the Great Blue Hole is a circle of deep indigo amid shallow water. It has become an extremely popular dive site since Jacques-Yves Cousteau stated that it was one of the best in the world.*

Inset: *One of the impressive limestone stalactites that can be found inside the Great Blue Hole.*

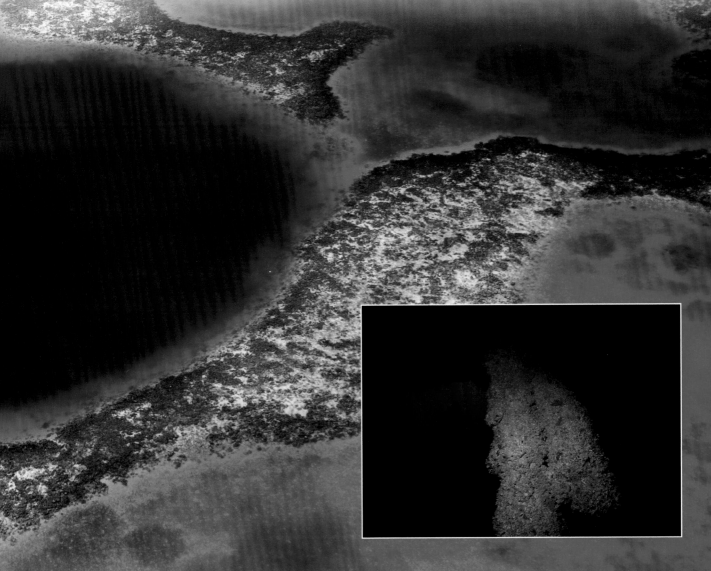

GREAT WALL OF CHINA

The Great Wall of China is one of the greatest construction projects ever undertaken by humankind and the longest wall ever built. It is one of the New Seven Wonders of the World. In total, with all branches included, it stretches over a distance of 8,852 kilometers (5,500 miles), crossing desert, grassland, mountains and plateaux in a great arc. It begins at the Hushan Great Wall in the east and passes through the provinces of Liaoning, Hebei, Beijing, Tianjin, Shanxi, Inner Mongolia, Ningxia, Shaanxi, Gansu and Qinghai to Jiayuguan Pass in the west.

Contrary to popular belief, the Great Wall is not a continuous, unbroken structure and neither was it built during one great effort. In fact, its length is interrupted by some short sections of trench, totaling 359.7 kilometers (223.5 miles) as well as natural defenses such as hills and rivers, which account for 2,232.5 kilometers (1,387.2 miles) of its overall span. Its earliest sections date back to between the 5th and 3rd centuries BC, a time of conflict between the Qi, Yan and Zhao states, each of which built walls of compacted earth and gravel to protect their borders. When Qin Shi Huang united China in 221 BC, becoming the first ruler of the Qin Dynasty, he ordered the walls that divided his empire to be destroyed, saving

only the sections that could be used as fortifications against the northern Xiongnu people - he ordered these walls to be extended. Unfortunately, no records remain of how far the Qin Dynasty wall stretched and most of the ancient sections of rammed earth have now disappeared. However, over the next 14 centuries, succeeding dynasties continued to shape, repair and extend the wall.

Much of what remains of the Great Wall of China, including its most famous stretches, were built during the Ming Dynasty (1368–1644), during a time when China was threatened by Mongolian and Manchurian tribes. The Ming wall is taller and stronger than its forebears – up to 7.6 meters (25 ft) high in places and between 4 and 9 meters (13–30 ft) thick – built of bricks and stone, and features watchtowers and barracks at regular intervals along its length. These would have been manned by up to a million soldiers defending the country from 'barbarian' invaders.

Another persistent popular belief has it that the Great Wall is the only human structure visible from the moon, but this is untrue; it is almost impossible to discern under perfect conditions even at a low orbit. However, it is, without doubt,

one of the greatest human achievements and one that cost countless lives in the making. Now a UNESCO World Heritage Site, it is a source of great cultural pride in China where its history is interwoven with colorful myths and legend. It is also one of the country's leading tourist destinations, attracting millions of visitors each year.

Main image: *At the westernmost point of the Great Wall is the ancient fortified city of Jiayuguan.*

Inset: *The restored section of the Great Wall, located at Badaling, is the most popular with tourists, and is only 80 kilometers (50 miles) from Beijing.*

HA LONG BAY

Ho Chi Minh described Ha Long Bay as 'the wonder that one cannot impart to others,' and, indeed, it is difficult to describe adequately this fabulous seascape made up of thousands of tall islands set in a dazzling blue sea. Its name translates as 'Bay of the Descending Dragons' and mythology has it that the islands were formed of the jewels and jade dropped from the mouths of dragons sent by the gods. It is a fitting legend and one that captures something of Ha Long Bay's magical beauty.

Located on the northeast coast of Vietnam in the Gulf of Tonkin, Ha Long Bay has an area of roughly 1,500 square kilometers (579 square miles). The islands that lend it such unique splendor are formed of limestone and schist, eroded over time into sheer columns etched by the sea and pierced with spectacular grottoes. Among the most famous, and visited, are Thien Cung (Heavenly Residence Grotto), Dau Go (Driftwood Grotto), Sung Sot (Surprise Grotto) and Tam Cung (Three Palace Grotto). Some islands have their own lakes while others are hollow, with vast interior caves filled with stalactites and stalagmites, and all are crowned with a profusion of tropical plant life, untouched since the vertical slopes make it extremely difficult to climb the island peaks. In fact, less than half have even been named. For those that have, the names are often based on what the island's shape was thought to

resemble. Typical examples are Voi Islet (elephant) and Ga Choi Islet (fighting cock). Some of the larger islands, however, have beautiful beaches and one or two even boast hotel resorts.

The area is not only famed for its magnificence, but is also an important archeological and botanical site. Simple tools and refuse heaps made up of discarded shells have been unearthed here and suggest that the area was one of the first places in the region to be settled by humans, around 20,000 years ago. The incredible plenty of Ha Long Bay's flora and fauna would have been an obvious draw for the primitive people. The same biodiversity is apparent now in the area's saltwater-flooded forests, evergreen tropical rainforest and coral reefs, which support thousands of different species.

In recognition of the area's immense scenic beauty and great biological interest, UNESCO pronounced Ha Long Bay a World Heritage Site in 1994. It remains one of Vietnam's biggest tourist attractions, and alongside the hotels and sunloungers, a small permanent population of about 1,600 people still live in small fishing villages. In some grottoes it is possible to find French graffiti dating back to the 19th century.

Main image: *An early morning mist settles over a fishing boat in Ha Long Bay.*

Inset: *Many of the limestone islands of Ha Long Bay are hollow and inside the caves are wondrous formations of stalactites and stalagmites.*

HAWAII VOLCANOES NATIONAL PARK

which rises 4,169 meters (13,677 ft) close to the center of the island – to the volcanic coastline where streams of fiery lava can be seen flowing into the ocean. The park is also home to Kilauea, which is in a state of constant eruption. Its cone vent, Puu Oo, dramatically spews hot magma from its peak and perfectly demonstrates how the destructive forces of nature can, simultaneously, provide pristine new land.

Located over 3,200 kilometers (2,000 miles) from the coast of California, in the Pacific Ocean, the Hawaiian islands are one of the world's most isolated island archipelagos. Its ecosystem boasts an exceptional variety of plants and animals, which rivals that of the Galapagos Islands. Hawaii Volcanoes National Park on Big Island boasts seven distinct ecological zones including sea coast, several types of woodland and rainforest where giant ferns grow, as well as the Ka'u Desert of volcanic ash and gravel. The park is also notable for stretches of black cooled lava flow from which the island is still being formed and contains some of Hawaii's most important archeological sites.

Covering an area of 1,309 square kilometers (505 sq miles), Hawaii's famous national park offers a landscape that seems to have been drawn from a South Seas adventure story. It stretches from Mauna Loa – the world's largest volcano,

The volcano craters were sacred to the indigenous Hawaiian people who would bring offerings to the goddess Pele.

As amazing a sight today as they were to the first Polynesian people who reached Hawaii around 400 AD, the volcanoes are undoubtedly the park's star attractions. They were first seen by European eyes when the British missionary William Ellis visited the island in 1823 with his American companion Asa Thurston. Ellis later recorded the wonder that the erupting volcano inspired in his journal, writing, a spectacle, sublime and even appalling, presented itself before us. We stopped and trembled. Astonishment and awe for some moments rendered us mute, and, like statues, we stood fixed to the spot, with our eyes riveted on the abyss below.' In fact, although the Kilauea, and one of the most active in the world, it is possible to hike to its rim and look down into the crater. Lava is mainly emitted from two vents, Puu Oo and Kupa'ianaha, and flows through a system of tubes about 12 kilometers (7.5 miles) to the shore at Wahhuala and Kamokuna. Since 1994, the lava has formed roughly 200 hectares (490 acres) of new land. Similar flows from an eruption in 1973 are already in the process of becoming vegetated, with tree ferns already growing there.

Today, the park is a UNESCO World Heritage Site and boasts a number of visitor centers and museums which cater to the large number of tourists who, like William Ellis, visit Hawaii's volcanoes and are awe-struck by the Earth's forces.

Main image: *Steam rises from Kilauea, Hawaii's most active – and visited – volcano. Local custom has it that the volcano erupts when the goddess Pele is angry.*

Inset: *Much of the lava that flows from Kilauea is spewed from the cone of Puu Oo, a cone vent on the volcano's flank.*

HIEROPOLIS-PAMUKKALE

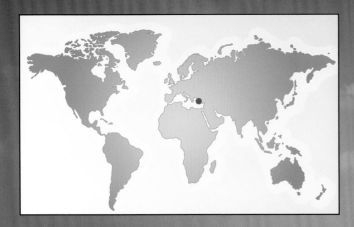

its petrified waterfalls and mineral forests, the 'white castle' of travertine (light-colored rock) terraces and naturally formed hot spring basins is dotted with Greek, Roman and Byzantine ruins, making it as historically fascinating as it is uniquely beautiful.

Located in the southwest of Turkey, the natural formations are known as Pamukkale (which means 'cotton castle'). The distinctive white hill or 'castle' is 2,700 meters (8,860 ft) long and 160 meters (524 ft) high and its broad travertine terraces are formed by the area's 17 hot water springs, which vary in temperature from 35 °C (95 °F) to 100 °C (212 °F). The mineral-heavy water flows from beneath the ground, depositing a calcium carbonate sediment, which in time solidifies to form travertine stone.

Hieropolis is an extraordinary, unearthly, place and a spa that has attracted people for thousands of years. With

At its crown is the ancient city of Hieropolis. Commonly thought to have been founded by Eumenes II, king of Pergamum

in the 2nd century BC, there is evidence to suggest that the site had already been occupied for several centuries. Originally Greek, the city passed to Roman rule and over time the hot spa baths that the site offered made Hieropolis a center of healing. It also played a role in the development of Christianity. Under the instruction of St. Paul, one of the religion's first churches was built here, while the city was also the last home of Christ's disciple Philip, who was crucified on the spot now occupied by a structure known as the Martyrium. From the 3rd century AD, the city's popularity increased hugely after a visit from Emperor Caracalla in 215 and it became an extremely popular retreat for the sick and elderly, attracting thousands of people each year, many of whom retired here.

As the city grew, new buildings were erected, including bath houses, a gymnasium and temples as well as homes for the citizens, theaters and streets dotted with the fountains and statues so treasured by Roman subjects. At its height, Hieropolis was a hub of art and philosophy, and a rich trade center with a population of around 100,000 citizens.

Sacked by Persian armies in the 7th century and later devastated by earthquakes, the glory of Hieropolis faded and by medieval times it was abandoned. However, in the mid-20th century archeologists began uncovering the city's ancient treasures from beneath the layer of limestone that had accumulated over the centuries. Today, it is once again a popular attraction where it is possible to swim in a hot spring among ancient stone relics. Declared a UNESCO World Heritage Site in 1988, Hieropolis-Pamukkale continues to delight visitors with its combination of incredible natural features and hot springs, as it has done for over 2,000 years.

Main image: *Time had taken its toll on the ancient theater at Hieropolis, but recent archeological works have unearthed many previously unseen statues and reliefs.*

Inset: *The sun-bleached travertine terraces of Pamukkale resemble frozen waterfalls.*

HOOVER DAM

the time it was finished, it was also a miracle of technology and engineering. No dam project of this scale had ever been attempted before and novel techniques and equipment had to be specially devised during construction.

The vast bulk of the Hoover Dam spans the Colorado River on the border of Arizona and Nevada, about 48 kilometers (30 miles) southeast of Las Vegas. Weighing a colossal 6 million tonnes (6.6 million tons), it created – and holds back – the 63,900 hectare (157,900 acre) Lake Mead, which stretches 180 kilometers (110 miles) behind the dam. On its completion in 1936 it was the world's largest hydroelectric dam and its 17 main turbines continue to produce roughly 4 billion kilowatt-hours of power every year for use in Nevada, Arizona and California.

Built with enough concrete to raise a solid tower 30 meters (100 ft) square to a height of 4 kilometers (2.5 miles) or lay a two-way road stretching from San Francisco to New York, the Hoover Dam is nothing less than monumental. At

Construction began on April 20, 1931, and finished – earlier than anticipated – on March 1, 1936. Before the dam itself could be built, the site had to be prepared. The Colorado River was diverted through four tunnels in the canyon walls and

the river bed dug out to expose solid bedrock. Because walls would also be bearing the weight of the dam, the cliffs were also excavated by men (called high-scalers) dangling on ropes from the rim of the canyon. With foundations made ready, the first concrete was poured on June 6, 1933, and involved a new process to help speed the curing process. Each section of concrete was threaded with narrow cooling pipes through which river water, and then refrigerated water, was poured. As each concrete block solidified, it contracted and the gaps were filled. Interestingly, the concrete is still curing to this day and continues to harden each year.

The dam was finished with architectural detailing in the Art Deco style by Gordon B. Kaufmann with Native American-inspired décor and artwork by artist Allen Tupper True. In all, 21,000 men worked on the dam. Housed in the specially built Boulder City, an average 3,500 toiled at the site each day.

In 1930, it was decided to name the dam after the sitting President, Herbert Hoover, who had been a great champion of the project from his time as Secretary of Commerce in the early 1920s. However, Hoover was unseated in 1932 by Franklin Delano Roosevelt and by the time it was completed, Roosevelt's

Secretary of the Interior Harold Ickes had reverted the name to the Boulder Dam. It wasn't until 1947 that the name changed again to honor President Hoover, as intended.

Today, the Hoover Dam is listed on the National Register of Historic Places and was also proclaimed a National Historic Landmark in 1985.

Main image: *Each year, millions of tourists come to marvel at the staggering immensity of the Hoover Dam, situated in the Black Canyon of the Colorado River.*

Inset: *The famous arch of the Hoover Dam is now a National Historic Landmark.*

Iguazu Falls

First Lady, Eleanor Roosevelt, is said to have exclaimed, 'Poor Niagara!'

In fact, though shorter and less wide than the Iguazu Falls, Niagara has a greater average rate of water spilling over its rim than Iguazu's 1,746 cubic meters per second (61,659 cu ft per second), yet what Iguazu lacks in terms of the volume of its torrent, it more than makes up for in beauty. Located on the border of Argentina and Brazil, at the center of two national parks, the falls stretch for 2.7 kilometers (1.67 miles) across the Iguazu River, and some are up to 82 meters (269 ft) high, significantly higher that Niagara's 52 meters (170 ft). The flow is broken by numerous islands on the edge of the waterfall, which prevent the falls taking the record for the longest curtain of water in the world but add to the startling splendor of the scenery.

Separating the Upper and Lower Iguazu rivers, the falls were created by volcanic activity which resulted in a great split in the earth, though local mythology claims that they were made by a jealous god who caught the woman he wished to marry

Cascading through pristine jungle, the 275 individual falls of the Iguazu Falls make up one of the grandest, most stunning, waterfall systems in the world. Indeed, they are so impressive that on seeing them for the first time US

escaping by boat with her mortal lover. In his fury, the god cracked the earth, forming the falls before the fleeing couple and dooming them to their deaths as they plummeted over the edge.

The most famous of the 275 individual falls is known as the 'Devil's Throat,' and is a horseshoe-shaped fall 150 meters (500 ft) across, while other particularly spectacular sights include the San Martin, Bossetti and Bernabe Mendez falls. As each tumbles into the lower river, a cloud of mist rises, creating permanent rainbows in the sunshine and dampening the leaves of the surrounding forest, making them a brilliant, iridescent green.

Hardly surprisingly, the Iguazu Falls are an extremely popular tourist destination (and have appeared in several movies) and the area is carefully managed to provide eco-friendly jungle trekking and amazing views from boardwalks. Together with the surrounding National Parks, the falls have been declared a World Heritage Site in recognition of the importance of the area's subtropical rainforest and their extraordinary natural beauty.

Main image: *The stunning natural beauty of the Iguazu Falls has led to them appearing in many popular films, including* Moonraker *and* Indiana Jones and the Crystal Skull.

Inset: *Derived from the Tupi words meaning 'big water,' the colossal falls are one of the largest waterfall systems in the world.*

INTERNATIONAL SPACE STATION

Bringing together the scientific expertise and technological resources of 16 nations around the world, the International Space Station (ISS) is, without doubt, the single most ambitious international scientific venture humankind has ever undertaken. Circling the Earth at a height of 390 kilometers (240 miles), the station is a floating laboratory devoted to human exploration of space and the largest manned satellite ever to orbit the planet.

The origins of the International Space Station project lie in the days of the Cold War, when both the United States and the USSR planned to put manned stations into orbit. Due to budget restraints in the US and political upheaval in the former Soviet Union, both the *Freedom* and *Mir* projects came close to being canceled, but in an unprecedented accord, made in 1992, presidents George Bush and Boris Yeltsin agreed to pool the resources of their respective nations. With

European countries, Canada and Japan also facing budgetary restrictions on their space programs, the project was expanded into a combined international effort.

The station is a modular structure and each new piece is fixed into position by astronauts working in space outside the station. Construction began on November 20, 1998, with the launch of the *Zarya* Control Module in a Russian rocket and

Main image: *As photographed from the space shuttle* Endeavor, *the International Space Station is seen against the blue and white surface of the Earth.*

Inset: *One of the most advanced service robots ever built, the ISS's robotic arm, named Dextre, reduces the need for space walks.*

Following pages: *The International Space Station, as seen from the Space Shuttle* Atlantis.

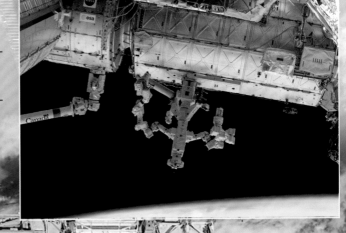

continued a fortnight later with the addition of a second module. Over the following months, the station continued to grow with new modules being carried from the surface by the Space Shuttles *Endeavor* and *Discovery*. In July 2000, a module known as *Zvezda* (Russian for 'star') was added which provided quarters for the first three-man crew, which arrived on November 2 of that year. Since then, the International Space Station has acquired solar arrays, logistics modules named *Leonardo* and *Raffaello*, a robot arm, an airlock and docking compartment. It has been staffed continuously since the first crew arrived and crew are replaced each three to six months.

Roughly the size of an American football pitch and measuring 73 meters by 108.5 meters (240 ft by 356 ft) and, the space station will be visible with the naked eye from Earth. Because the International Space Station travels around the planet at an average speed of 27,743.8 kilometers per hour (17,239.2 mph) – which gives astronauts aboard 16 sunrises and sunsets each day – it is only visible for short periods to those standing in the right place, but appears as the brightest object in the night sky. To help those who wish to witness history in the making, NASA publish a schedule on their website showing the times it can be seen from many cities around the world and where to look.

ISTANBUL

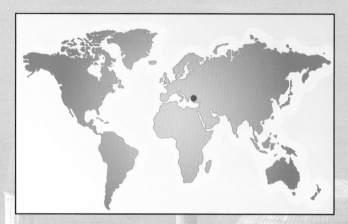

A vibrant city built at the point where East meets West, Istanbul has a long and fascinating history, stretching back thousands of years. During that time, it has played an important role in world history as the capital of empires and the modern city of Istanbul has inherited a golden architectural heritage that reflects the varied styles of the cultures which have held power here. These historic treasures

Opposite page: *The Hagia Sophia, meaning 'Holy Wisdom,' was the largest cathedral in the world for almost a millennia.*

Below: *Construction of Topkapi Palace began in 1459 and it was the official home of the Ottoman sultans for 400 years.*

give the city a unique, cosmopolitan character found nowhere else on Earth.

There is evidence to suggest that Istanbul's site has been inhabited since about 6700 BC, the city of Byzantion was founded on the Bosphorus Strait, which separates Europe and Asia, by Greek colonists in 667 BC. Although little evidence now remains of the Ancient Greeks who once lived here, the Maiden's Tower (or Leander's Tower as it is sometimes known) can be seen on a small islet in the strait. Originally built by an Athenian general called Alcibiades in 408 BC, the tower has been rebuilt and restored many times and is still in use today.

Conquered by the Romans in 196 AD, and renamed as the Latinized 'Byzantium,' the city became the capital of the Roman Empire under Constantine the Great in 330, and was renamed again, this time as Constantinople, an event commemorated by the erection of the Column of Constantine in the city center. When the Roman Empire was partitioned into East and West, Constantinople remained as the capital of the Eastern Roman (Byzantine) Empire and was a wealthy center of trade as well as the political heart of the empire. During the 1,000 year Byzantine period, the city saw new wonders being raised, including the Hagia Sophia, which was then the largest cathedral in the world (and later to become a mosque), by 360. Unfortunately, little now remains of the Great Palace of Constantine or the enormous Hippodrome he had built, though Byzantine relics can still be found across the city.

When Constantinople fell to the Ottoman Turks in 1453 a new age of construction began. The Ottomans built the vast and delicately ornate Topkapi Palace to house the Sultan as well as many superb mosques, including the Faith Mosque on the site of the Byzantine Church of the Holy Apostles (which was demolished to make way for it), and the elaborately domed Blue Mosque, now one of the city's most famous sights.

The Republic of Turkey was founded in 1923, and in the following years Istanbul (officially renamed in 1930) suffered as the Turkish capital moved to Ankara and some of the city's historic buildings were torn down to make way for new boulevards. Nevertheless, the wonders that remain offer a vivid reminder of the city's glorious past. Istanbul's historic districts were placed on the list of UNESCO World Heritage Sites in 1985 and the city became the joint European Capital for Culture in 2010.

ITAIPU DAM

Supplying more electricity than ten nuclear power stations, the Itaipu Dam is the world's second largest hydroelectric power facility (China's Three Gorges Dam is the biggest) and one of the American Society of Civil Engineers' Seven Wonders of the Modern World.

Straddling the Paraná River that forms the border between Brazil and Paraguay, the Itaipu Dam is the result of a groundbreaking agreement to share the river's electricity-producing potential made between the two countries and signed on July 22, 1966. Built between January 1975 and October 1982 (though the final two electricity generating units did not begin operating until 1991) the dam is one of the biggest – and most expensive – construction projects undertaken.

Before building even began, about 10,000 families had to be relocated to make room for the new 170-kilometer (106-mile) long lake that would eventually be formed by the dam and the course of the world's seventh largest river diverted.

Over 45 million tonnes (50 million tons) of earth and rock were then excavated; the dam itself was built using enough steel and iron to create 380 Eiffel Towers and enough concrete to build 15 cross-Channel Eurotunnels. In total, roughly 40,000 people worked on it and the final cost was US$27 billion.

The finished structure stretches 7.76 kilometers (4.82 miles), reaching a height of 196 meters (643 ft), and holding back 26 billion tonnes (29 billion tons) of water. In effect, the complete dam is actually made up of four segments: a rock fill dam, an earth fill dam, the main concrete dam and a concrete wing dam. The 20 generating units (comprising turbine and generator, of which 18 are in operation at any one time) combine to create an average of 75 billion kilowatts of power each year, enough to supply 78 percent of Paraguay's power needs and 25 percent of Brazil's. An oil-fired power station would require 536,000 barrels of oil per day to produce the same amount of energy. The Itaipu Dam does so without producing any carbon emissions.

Although it may lack the Art Deco grace of the Hoover Dam, the Itaipu Dam is undeniably one of humankind's most impressive achievements and represents a great success for the two countries that shared in its construction. Since completion, it has attracted millions of visitors from across the world as well as inspiring the American composer Philip Glass to write a piece of music in its honor.

Main image: *Currently the world's second largest hydroelectric dam, the Itaipu is shared by the governments of Brazil and Paraguay.*

Inset: *One of the manmade channels that connect the Itaipu Dam to the Paraná River. These waterways have become popular locations for watersports.*

ITSUKUSHIMA SHRINE

Appearing to float on the sea at high tide, the buildings of the Itsukushima Shrine are an integral part of the tranquil, unspoiled landscape of Miyajima island in Japan. A Shinto holy site since the reign of the Empress Suiko in the 6th century AD, the shrine has been destroyed and rebuilt many times over the years and has been considered one of the Three Views of Japan – the most beautiful and iconic sights in the country – since the mid 17th century.

Located on the island formally named Itsukushima, but more commonly know as Miyajima, which translates as 'Shrine Island', the Itsukushima Shrine is a complex of buildings that are widely held to represent a pinnacle of Japanese architecture. Built to honor the three daughters of Susano-o no Mikoto, the Shinto god of the sea, the complex is built out over the water on a pier that extends elegantly into the bay. For many years the land itself was considered too holy to be desecrated by buildings and commoners could only approach the shrine by sea. Later, when the island became inhabited, it was forbidden to the sick, while giving birth and burying the dead were also prohibited. Even today, the island has no cemeteries or hospitals.

The most famous of the shrine's structures is the striking *torii* gate, which is roughly 16 meters (52 ft) high with a width of 22.3 meters (73 ft). At high tide, it appears to be rising from the water as a reminder to pilgrims passing beneath that they are entering a sacred area. On the pier itself are beautifully proportioned buildings that blend harmoniously with the landscape, including a prayer hall, noh theater stage and main hall, all connected by boardwalks. The *torii* gate and the main buildings are each painted a vibrant vermilion, which creates a contrast with the blue of the water and the green of Mount Misen behind, perfectly demonstrating the Japanese notion of architectural beauty: a thoughtful combination of nature and human ingenuity.

Now a UNESCO World Heritage Site, the shrine – and others that are found close by – has been attracting visitors for centuries. The first shrine on the site was founded in 593 AD, and the present design built in 1168. Various natural disasters, including typhoons and mud slides, have damaged the buildings on numerous occasions and the present complex dates to 1571 when it was last rebuilt to the 12th century plan. Still one of Japan's most stunningly scenic places, and one that is rich in history and folklore, Itsukushima Shrine is considered to be one of the country's greatest national treasures.

Main image: *When the tide draws back from the base of Itsukushima's torii gate, visitors wade through the mud to place coins in cracks in the wood and make a wish.*

Inset: *Apart from the torri gate, the Itsukushima Shrine has many other well preserved buildings.*

JEITA GROTTO

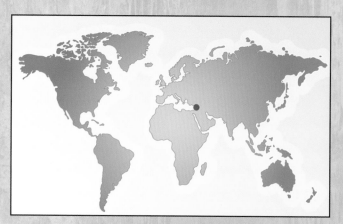

Containing the world's largest stalactite, the Jeita Grotto is an underground system of caves adorned with fantastic limestone formations. It stretches for 9 kilometers (5.6 miles) into the Lebanon Mountains. Comprising of two levels called the upper and lower galleries – the lower is the source of the Nahr al-Kalb River, which flows through it, giving visitors the opportunity to glide by boat through this otherworldly, subterranean wonderland.

Located in the Nahr al-Kalb Valley about 18 kilometers (11 miles) north of the Lebanese capital Beirut, the caves of the Jeita Grotto are the most extensive in the country, and contain some of the most spectacular, and most beautiful, limestone formations in the world. The upper cave is the shorter of the two galleries with an overall length of 2.2 kilometers (1.37 miles), of which just under 750 meters (half a mile) can be explored on foot. Throughout, its spaces are crowded with a dizzying display of natural limestone structures, including columns, draped 'frozen waterfalls' of stone and mushroom-like protuberances as well as stalagmites and stalactites. Sinkholes and chasms drop to depths of 100 meters (330 ft). Close to the entrance are three vast, cathedral like spaces with ceilings reaching 120 meters (390 ft) above the cavern floor. The first two of these are called the White Chamber and the Red Chamber respectively due to the color of the formations. In the first chamber these have been created with pure, white calcite, while in the second a small amount of iron oxide has

naturally mixed with the calcite, giving the stones a rusty red tint. The White Chamber also contains the longest stalactite in the world, which measures 8.2 meters (27 ft).

About 60 meters (200 ft) below, and joined by a walkway, is the lower cave, which is 6.2 kilometers (3.85 miles) long, though only 500 meters (1,640 ft) are accessible to visitors. Here the smooth waters of the river are interrupted by large waterfalls and rapids as they flow through a succession of caverns, again adorned with limestone formations.

While the caverns were inhabited by humans in prehistoric times, the lower galleries were rediscovered by an American missionary in 1836. Since then, successive explorers have pushed further back into the system, discovering the upper chambers as recently as 1958, the same year that the caves were opened to the public. In recent times, the beautiful Jeita Grotto has become a national icon of Lebanon and now attracts hundreds of thousands of visitors each year.

Opposite page: *The Jeita Grotto cave complex is composed of an upper and a lower cave carved out of the Jurassic limestone. It contains spectacular rock formations.*

Right: *In the upper chambers of the Jeita Grotto is the world's longest stalactite.*

JERUSALEM

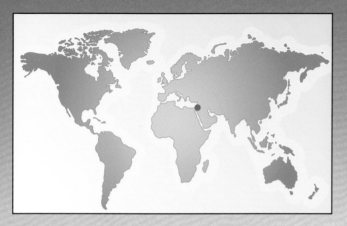

of great antiquity, co-exist with the buildings of a thriving modern city, it is the home of many sites of great religious significance. Steeped in history, in spirituality and in mythology, Jerusalem is a unique and awe-inspiring place.

While evidence suggests that the site where Jerusalem now stands has been occupied by humans since the copper age, archeologists believe that the history of the city proper begins in about 2600 BC. Jewish lore relates that the city was founded by forebears of Abraham and became the capital of the Jewish Nation of Israel under King David around 1000 BC. The city later came under the rule of numerous invaders and has a heritage that is as full of conflict as it is of events that have shaped world history.

Now a UNESCO World Heritage Site, the Old City at Jerusalem's heart is a relatively small area of 0.9 square

With a history stretching back over 6,000 years, Jerusalem is one of the world's most venerable cities and a holy place to three of humanity's greatest religions: Judaism, Christianity and Islam. Here architectural treasures

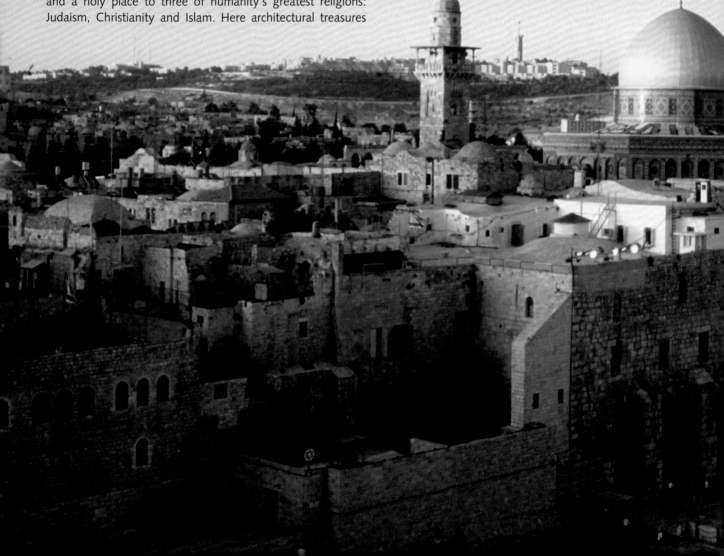

kilometer (0.35 sq mile), encompassed by Byzantine-era walls, which comprised the entire city until the 19th century. It is split into Muslim, Christian, Armenian and Jewish quarters, each of which is redolent of Jerusalem's diverse heritage and it also contains many of the city's most holy sites. Comprising a significant portion of the Old City is Temple Mount where God is said to have created Adam and Solomon's Temple once stood with its Holy of Holies protecting the Ark of the Covenant. The mount is now home to the Dome on the Rock, an important Islamic shrine dating to 692 AD and built over the Foundation Stone, the most holy of Jewish sites as well as having great significance for Muslims as the place where the Prophet Muhammad ascended to Heaven.

Elsewhere on Temple Mount is the Western (Wailing) Wall which dates to around 20 BC and the days of Herod the Great. It was once part of the Second Temple complex, built to replace Solomon's Temple which was destroyed by the Babylonians around 587 BC and itself destroyed by a Roman army in 70 AD. Another site of major historical and religious importance within the Old City is the Church of the Holy Sepulchre, which is said to have been built over Golgotha, the hill where Christ was crucified, and the place where he was interred and resurrected. Replacing a temple dedicated to the Roman goddess Venus that had been constructed in the 2nd century AD, the Church of the Holy Sepulchre was begun in 325 AD on the command of the Roman Emperor Constantine.

Throughout the city are other remains, monuments, shrines, churches, synagogues and mosques too numerous to mention but all of which help shroud Jerusalem with a unique character. Impossible to capture in words, the city's atmosphere is suffused with age and the intermingled histories of numerous cultures. It is also an important archeological site, and a city of outstanding beauty.

Main image: *The faithful gather at the Wailing Wall in Jerusalem, situated in the shadow of the Omar Mosque.*

Inset: *One of the most significant sites in Christianity, the Mount of Olives is where Christ is said to have ascended to Heaven.*

KARST FORMATIONS OF GUILIN

Lending the scenery around the city of Guilin an unexpected – almost alien – beauty, the region's craggy limestone peaks, strewn across flat plains, are inextricably bound up with the China of popular imagination. Densely vegetated and riddled with caves, they form a magical landscape that seems drawn directly from a story book and one that is recognizable from countless paintings and photographs. So stunning is the landscape here that the Chinese have an old saying, 'Guilin's scenery is best among all under heaven.'

Covering an area of over 5,180 square kilometers (2,000 sq miles) in the northeast of the Guangxi Zhuang

Autonomous Region in the south of China, the spectacular peaks of the Guilin area are one of China's most popular tourist destinations. These jagged, angular rock formations are a superb example of karstification, a process, which takes place over many millions of years and sees soluble bedrock (in this case limestone) being dissolved by mildly acidic water, which results in the sculpture of strange formations on the surface and extensive cave systems below ground. Although there are many examples of karstification around the world, other aspects of Guilin's geology and geography (such as the formation of the Himalayas, relatively close by) have combined to form a landscape like no other: a landscape that is dominated by the green peaks. Pierced by sinkholes, caverns and grottoes such as Reed Flute Cave – home to stunning limestone pillars, stalactites and stalagmites – below ground the scenery is often just as extraordinary.

Among the area's other highlights is Seven Star Park, which boasts, on Putuo Hill, a 22-storey temple and the Seven Stars Cave with its underground waterfall. Elsewhere is Elephant Trunk Hill, so named because it resembles an elephant drinking from the river. Threading its way through the hills is the Li River, which offers an excellent way for visitors to view the scenery. While archeologists believe that it has been home to humans for some 30,000 years, today, the landscape around the neat city of Guilin seems almost untouched. Small villages dot the landscape and life here goes on as it has done for centuries.

Hardly surprisingly, the area's phenomenal natural beauty has inspired poetry and literature throughout the ages. Here and there, carved into the limestone in caves and beneath overhangs, are poems dating back over 200 years. More recently the area has also attracted the attention of movie directors; the karst formations of Guilin starred as the scenery of the planet Kashyyyk in *Star Wars III: Revenge of the Sith*.

Main image: *The view from the top of Moon Hill gives an unparalleled view across the karst formations of Guilin's landscape.*

Inset: *Reed Flute Cave boasts many unique rock formations, including limestone structures known as Crystal Palace, Dragon Pagoda and Virgin Forest.*

Following pages: *The fantastical karst peaks of Guilin form a stunning backdrop to the River Li at dawn.*

KHAJURAHO

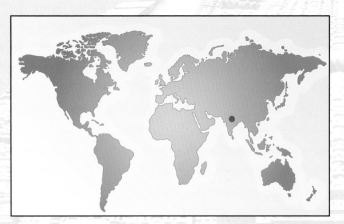

The largest of the temples is the Kandariya Mahadeo, which rises over 31 meters (100 ft) and is a shrine dedicated to Lord Shiva – the supreme god in Shiva Hindu lore. Other notable temples include the Chitragupta, with its impressive 1.5-meter (5-ft) statue of the sun god Surya driving a chariot and the partially ruined Chaunsat, dedicated to the goddess Kali – who presides over the passing of time and eternal change – which is thought to be the oldest of the temples.

Today, the temple complex of Khajuraho is one of India's most visited places, and a UNESCO World Heritage Site. An open air archeological museum displays statues and relics of those temples that are now ruined.

Opposite page: *Built with lofty domes and spires, Khajuraho's temple buildings are airy and light and lavishly festooned with detailed carvings.*

Below: *The Kandariya Mahadeo is one of the best preserved of the temples and its stepped spire is thought to represent Mount Meru, Shiva's holy mountain.*

Dedicated to the Hindu and Jain religions, and steeped in legend, the 22 temples of Khajuraho are intricately carved architectural masterpieces. Perhaps most famous for the erotic sculptures that are included among the scenes of everyday life on the facades of the temples, it is a common misconception that most, if not all, of the carvings are sexual in nature. In fact, only about 10 percent depict amorous scenes and the remainder serve as a vivid exhibition of life at the peak of the Khajuraho's cultural importance. Although archeologists and historians often disagree about the purpose of the sculptures, there is no doubting their magnificent artistry.

The small town of Khajuraho is in the Indian state of Madhya Pradesh, at the center of northern India, and dates back over a thousand years to the time of the Chandela dynasty that held sway in the region from the 10th century AD until the 13th. Considered by many to represent the peak of India's architectural achievement during the Medieval age, there were originally 85 temples, built between about 950 and 1050. Today, only 22 remain, but stand testament to their creators' genius.

The temples were all built of sandstone and, unusually, no mortar was used to hold the blocks together. Instead, the masons used a highly precise method of mortise and tenon joints that help to make the temples look as if they have each been carved from a single giant piece of rock. Outside, the sculpture largely depicts scenes of Indian life. Apart from erotic displays, other figures are putting on make-up, playing instruments, farming, making pots and going about other everyday tasks. The sexual gymnastics, which appear to illustrate scenes from the *Kama Sutra*, are usually kept at some distance from the carvings of deities. Inside, the carvings are more calm and respectful. To walk through one of the temples' east-facing grand entranceways is to leave behind the bustle of earthly life depicted on the exterior. Stepped ceilings are decorated with carved flowers and geometric designs.

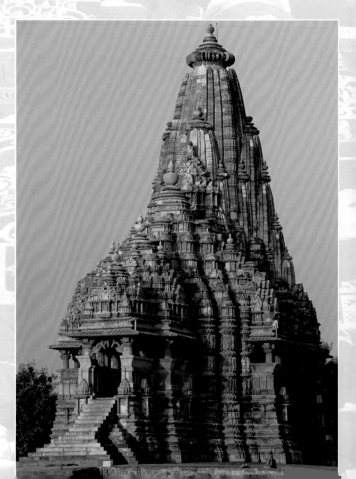

KILIMANJARO

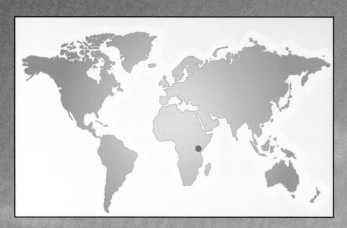

Africa, from afar the snow-capped mountain rises like a mirage from heat-baked lands just 340 kilometers (210 miles) south of the equator.

Located at the heart of its own National Park, which is also a UNESCO World Heritage Site, Mount Kilimanjaro lies to the northeast of Tanzania, close to the Kenyan border. While the origins of its name are not fully understood, it is thought that it derives from two local languages. In Swahili the word *Kilima* means 'mountain' while *Njaro* is the Kichagga word for 'white.'

The mountain began forming about a million years ago and is volcanic. In fact, it has three peaks, each of which is a volcanic cone. The highest of these is Kibo, which is also the site of Kilimanjaro's highest point: Uhuru Peak, which rises from the

Africa's highest mountain, and the world's highest free-standing peak, Mount Kilimanjaro's summit rises 5,895 meters (19,340 ft) above the savannah. Providing some of the most famous, and photographed, views to be found in

crater's rim. Further down are the Mawenzi and Shira cones, which reach heights of 5,149 meters (16,893 ft) and 3,962 meters (13,000 ft) respectively. While Kilimanjaro is classed as a dormant volcano there are still signs of activity in the Kibo crater and its last eruption was just 200 years ago.

At various heights Kilimanjaro supports five distinct ecosystems. Its lower slopes were once home to unbroken dense rainforest, but the conditions are excellent for farming – particularly on Kilimanjaro's southern flanks, which receive more rainfall – and are now home to numerous smallholdings growing coffee and vegetables. Above is a forest zone which encircles the mountain between the heights of roughly 1,800 to 2,800 meters (6,000 to 9,000 ft) and gives way to a band of low-growing shrubs and heather at higher altitudes. Beyond 4,200 meters (14,000 ft) is alpine desert where few plants can be found and the summit is a snowfield, with glaciers, freezing temperatures and oxygen levels which are about half that at the base. The lower ecosystems are home to a variety of birds and animals, including brightly colored birds such as the Hornbill and Turaco as well as blue and colobus monkeys, small antelopes and leopards.

The first recorded ascent of Kilimanjaro took place in 1889 when the local 18-year-old guide Yohana Kinyala Lawuo led the German geographer Hans Meyer and Austrian mountaineer Ludering Purtscheller to the summit. Today, about 25,000 people per year attempt the climb which is, despite the mountain's apparently gentle slope, more punishing than might be thought due to the cold and lack of oxygen at higher altitudes.

Main image: *The snow capped summit of Mount Kilimanjaro rises above dense, low cloud.*

Inset: *Various ecosystems are supported on Kilimanjaro's flanks, ranging from tropical jungle to alpine meadows, glaciers and snowfields at the summit.*

KREMLIN AND RED SQUARE

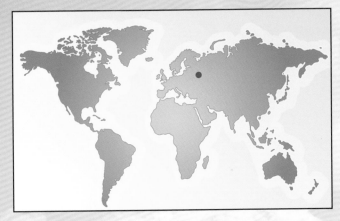

The Moscow Kremlin complex and Red Square, at the heart of Moscow, have taken a central role in Russian culture again and again over the years. Here, events that have shaped Russian, and world, history have played out. The Kremlin has served as the home of tzars and presidents including Lenin and Stalin while Red Square is not only commonly seen as the hub of Moscow but of all Russia. Surrounded by some of its most important and celebrated buildings – not only the Kremlin itself,

but the bright onion domes of St. Basil's Cathedral, Lenin's Mausoleum, Kazan Cathedral and the State History Museum – the great square seems to reflect the sheer scale of the Russian landscape and its surrounding buildings the glories of the country's achievements.

The Kremlin is a fortified complex of buildings that has been remodeled and added to many times over the centuries. It lies on a site that has been occupied since about the 2nd century BC and within its turreted walls today are four palaces and four cathedrals. The early wooden fort was replaced by a citadel, as well as cathedrals and monastery buildings, under the rule of Ivan I in the 14th century and was renovated using architects from Renaissance Italy by Grand Prince Ivan III (Ivan the Great), in the late 15th and early 16th centuries. Those building works also called for the creation of Red Square, and all buildings within 234 meters (767 ft) of the Kremlin's eastern wall were razed. Originally called 'the Great Market,' it was not until the mid 17th century that the square became known by its modern name, which derives from the color of the brickwork around it. The proximity of the Moskva River saw the square become a hub of commerce in the growing city and over the years it became a place for Moscow to

celebrate with pageants and parades. By the late 16th century it had also acquired a platform from which royal proclamations were read.

As the centuries passed, Red Square and the Kremlin saw many major events unfold: monarchs were crowned, in 1812 Napoleon Bonaparte and the French armies took the city and attempted to destroy the Kremlin and Red Square became a symbol of Soviet power after the Russian Revolution. Buildings were renovated in new styles and others, such as the Grand Kremlin Palace and the 242-meter (794-ft) length of the Upper Trading Rows (which later became the famous GUM Department Store), were built.

Red Square and the Kremlin are now a UNESCO World Heritage Site. Their awe-inspiring structures and monuments, as well as the sense of being at the center of Russian history, draws millions of visitors each year. Today, as for many centuries, the area remains one of the nation's great treasures and at the heart of Russia's cultural heritage.

Main image: *Behind the Kremlin's red turreted walls is a complex of gardens, cathedrals and palaces built and restored over centuries. To the left is the Great Kremlin Palace (with the green roof), built for Nikolai I in 1849.*

Inset: *The view looking over the brightly colored domes of St. Basil's Cathedral (with St. Savior's Tower behind) to Red Square.*

LA SAGRADA FAMILIA

Perhaps one of the most ambitious – and long-running – undertakings of modern times, the fantastical, many-spired cathedral of La Sagrada Familia in Barcelona has been an ongoing project since 1882. With a unique design that is as

---

Opposite page: *La Sagrada Familia's completion date is estimated to be 2026 – 144 years after the first plans were drawn.*

Below: *A detail of La Sagrada Familia's carvings and art-glass windows. The entire building has an eccentric beauty that is unique to Gaudi's masterpiece.*

impressive at it is unusual, finished or not the cathedral has long been one of the world's most striking works of architecture.

Originally assigned to the architect Francesco del Villar in 1882, he resigned the commission a year later and the design was handed over to the famed Catalan architect, Antoni Gaudi. Gaudi devoted the final 15 years of his life to the cathedral's construction, living in a workshop on the site and forsaking any other projects. After his unexpected death in 1926 – he was run over by a tram – the mantle passed on to Domènech Sugranyes who continued Gaudi's work until the outbreak of the Spanish Civil War in 1936. Since that time, several well known teams of architects have endeavored to make Gaudi's original vision a reality.

When Gaudi designed the church, he stated that it should be the 'last great sanctuary of Christendom.' Indeed, every façade, room and the roof of the edifice are adorned with Christian symbolism – even the 18 spindle-shaped towers that adorn the roof represent the 12 apostles, the Virgin Mary, the four evangelists and – the tallest tower – Jesus Christ. The Nativity façade, located on the eastern wall, was completed in 1935 and bears all the hallmarks of Gaudi's unique design. The Passion, on the west, is particularly moving in its portrayal of Christ's torment on the Cross. The final façade, planned for the southern exterior wall, is to be named The Glory and is not yet ready for exhibition.

While Gaudi intended the outside of the church to represent Christ's human life on Earth, with all the pain and suffering that involved, he wanted the interior of the building to represent his celestial home. The inside of the cathedral is a haven of beauty, peace and tranquility. Being a staunch nationalist, Gaudi also planned to have parts of the church dedicated to individual regions of Spain.

These days, despite being unfinished La Sagrada Familia is one of Barcelona's most popular tourist attractions. Visitors to the cathedral can climb a spiral staircase up into the Nativity or Passion towers and enjoy unrivaled views of the city. The nave, the museum and the crypt are also open to visitors. The final completion date for the church is currently set for 2026, yet many local architects are fighting for a cessation in the building work, so that they can refer to Gaudi's original designs and remain true to his vision.

LEANING TOWER OF PISA

While the reason for its widespread fame is unlikely to have pleased the tower's original designer, there is no doubting that Pisa's leaning tower is an international icon. Tilting 3.99 degrees to the southeast, which puts its roof at 3.9 meters (12 ft 10 in) from the vertical, the tower is an architectural masterpiece though it has become a symbol of poor workmanship.

Standing, awkwardly, in the Italian city of Pisa's cathedral square, the Leaning Tower of Pisa, or *La Torre di Pisa*, as it is properly known, was designed as an unattached bell tower for the cathedral. Its inadequate foundations were dug in 1173 to a depth of less than 3 meters (10 ft) in unstable soil and construction took place over the next two centuries in three phases. The first floor was built in a 'blind arcade' style, in which reliefs of columns are applied to the outer wall, echoing the upper floors. By the time that builders had reached the third floor in 1178, however, it was apparent that the tower had begun to tilt and building work was stopped. Almost 100 years later, the architect Giovanni di Simone was hired to complete the building and, rather than pulling it down and starting again, he continued to build upward, constructing subsequent floors slightly higher on one side to counteract the tilt. A careful inspection reveals that the tower is, in fact, very slightly curved.

Completed to the seventh floor by 1319, the final element – the bell chamber – was added in 1372 by the architect Tommaso di Pisano who, again, attempted to counteract the

tower's angle by building the crowning chamber with one side higher than the other.

The result is a distinctively quirky, if architecturally fine, building that over the centuries has become recognized around the world. Just under 57 meters (186 ft) high on the side furthest from the ground, it has a diameter of a little under 15.5 meters (50 ft 10 in) at the base and, until relatively recently, a much greater tilt of 5.5 degrees. By the 1960s the extent of the tower's lean had begun to cause concern, leading to a conference of international mathematicians, architects and engineers who were tasked with stopping the famous tower from toppling. In 1990, the tower was attached to supporting cables at the third floor, tonnes of soil were dug from beneath the raised side, and it was pulled back into the same position it had occupied in the early 19th century. The process was repeated in 2008 and the foundations strengthened further. Now, the tower has stopped moving for the first time since the 12th century and it is hoped that this great landmark will be safe for at least the next five centuries.

Opposite page: *Today, the Leaning Tower of Pisa is one of Italy's most visited tourist destinations. It is a UNESCO World Heritage Site along with surrounding monuments, including the cathedral itself.*

Right: *A detail of the ornate, circular Gothic arcades that adorn the exterior of the Leaning Tower of Pisa.*

MACHU PICCHU

Situated 2,430 meters (7,970 ft) above sea level, hidden in a dense Peruvian rainforest between the two summits of Huayna Picchu and Machu Picchu, after which the city was named, are the ancient ruins often referred to as 'The Lost City of the Incas.' Swathed in mist and surrounded by jagged peaks, the fabulous and majestic city is a reminder of the achievements of the Incan people.

Machu Picchu was built at the height of the Incan Empire, around 1450 AD. Unfortunately, the city was not destined to be inhabited for long: it is believed that by 1572 the entire population was wiped out by a smallpox epidemic, brought to Peruvian shores by conquering Spanish forces. Although the Conquistadors subdued much of the Incan culture and routinely defaced or destroyed the temples and sacred stones of the indigenous people, it is not thought they ever

reached Machu Picchu, as many of the original buildings remained undamaged.

The purpose of the citadel is much argued over. Some scholars believed it belonged to the Incan emperor Pachacuti and served as his mountain retreat, while another theory speculates that it may have been an agricultural center, testing the viability of different crops as the size and location of the terraces in Machu Picchu are only suitable for small-scale farming.

The remains of the citadel are split between urban and agricultural sections with a wall separating the two. The agricultural area is terraced, which not only provided more accessible farmland to the inhabitants but also protection; potential attackers would have to climb up high walls leaving themselves vulnerable. The main buildings of the urban section are built in the classic Incan style called *ashlar*. The Incans used polished, uniformly shaped stones and slotted them together without the use of mortar. They were undoubted experts in the technique and the buildings in the center of the city are so perfectly constructed that not even a blade of grass can be pushed between the stones.

The 140 remaining structures include temples, sanctuaries, parks, thatched houses and fountains. Machu Picchu also has an Intihuatana stone, often referred to as 'The Hitching Post of the Sun.' Historians believe these stones were thought to tie the sun to the earth.

Considering its protected position, it is unsurprising that this jewel of ancient Incan civilization lay undisturbed for many years. In fact, it was not until 1911 that American historian Hiram Bingham was led to the site by a local boy. Bingham, who had actually been searching for the Incan city of Vilcapampa, realized its importance and immediately began archeological studies. Today, Machu Picchu is Peru's most popular tourist destination and a UNESCO World Heritage Site.

Main image: *The stunning views of Machu Picchu. The city dates back to the mid-15th century and is thought to have had religious significance.*

Inset: *Often swathed in clouds, Machu Picchu's terraces provided level agricultural ground and steep walls that would have made attacking the city difficult.*

MALDIVES

The most scattered nation on the planet – the total land mass is just 300 square kilometers (116 sq miles) – the Republic of the Maldives is also the smallest of Asian countries, and the lowest country in the world, with a highest point of just 2.3 meters (7 ft 7 in) above sea level. Today, the Maldives has a population of about 300,000, a number which is supplemented by approximately 70,000 foreigners, most of whom work in the tourism industry. The capital is Malé, which has a population of just over 100,000. Most of the nation's native people live on just 185 of the islands, with many of the remainder being occupied by single-resort tourist facilities. Many others are used for agriculture or are uninhabited and completely pristine.

While it may be a small nation, in terms of beauty and climate the Republic of the Maldives is one of the most fortunate. For the most part protected from the ocean by reefs and lagoons, the island's characteristic white beaches are washed by lapping clear waters. The average temperature varies little, between 24° C (75° F) and 33° C (91° F) throughout the year, and soft ocean breezes usually stir the humid air, though the islands are visited annually by fierce tropical monsoons. The islands are also one of the world's favorite scuba diving sites. Offshore are living coral gardens inhabited by more than 2,000 species

The 1,190 coral islands of the Maldives are strewn like an emerald necklace across 90,000 square kilometers (34,750 sq miles) of the Indian Ocean. Sitting atop 26 separate atolls, their palm fringed, white sandy beaches, lagoons and turquoise waters offer the archetypal tropical island paradise.

Lying in a double-chain formation along a ridge that ascends from the floor of the Indian Ocean, the Maldive Islands stretch across the Equator off the southwest of India's southern tip.

of sea life, including endangered species, brightly colored reef fish and the rare whale shark.

Unfortunately, these beautiful islands are threatened by climate change. Since the beginning of the 20th century, sea levels have risen about 20 centimeters (8 in) and the fact that the islands are so low-lying puts them at particular risk of further rises. So serious is the problem, that the republic's government has begun buying up land in India, in case it should become necessary to move the population. Such an event would be a tragic loss, but for the moment the islands remain one of the world's most serene and beautiful destinations, attracting over 600,000 tourists each year.

Main image: *The 1,190 islands of the Maldives include numerous tiny islets. Fringed by clear waters, coral reefs and white beaches, about 200 are uninhabited and completely unspoiled.*

Inset: *The islands rise from atolls of live coral and sand that are at the summit of a ridge which runs for 965 kilometers (600 miles) through the Indian Ocean.*

MARRAKECH

Once the capital of the Saadian dynasty, Marrakech is a hot, fevered, labyrinthine city that assaults the senses. Within its covered marketplaces and twisting alleyways the visitor enters a world of snake charmers and belly dancers, laden with the scent of spices and food cooking in the open air. A world where traders haggle over handmade leather and silver jewelry and donkey carts clatter through narrow streets; a world where it is possible to find respite in cool and richly ornamented courtyards or sweat in steamy hammam spas, and where palaces and grand gateways recall the opulence of the sultans.

Located to the southwest of Morocco, at the base of the Atlas mountains, Marrakech is a teeming city where modern and ancient meet. Often called the 'Red City' for the color of its brickwork, Marrakech centers on the Djemaa el Fna, in the medina quarter: the old part of the city. Presided over by the impressive Koutoubia minaret (the city's largest mosque, which dates to the 12th century), the Djemaa el Fna is a dizzying, bustling *souk* (marketplace) during the day, but as night falls the square becomes a combination of open-air restaurants, cafés and performance spaces, where Chleuh boys dance to traditional Berber music alongside story-tellers, acrobats, snake charmers and magicians. In fact, recognition of the square's great cultural importance to Morocco's traditional performance arts prompted UNESCO to begin a new program, which listed world sites declared Masterpieces of the Oral and Intangible Heritage of Humanity.

Beyond the Djemaa el Fna square, Marrakech's medina district is a maze of twisting alleyways, which often seem untouched by time or Western culture. Outside artisans' workshops and small shops are street vendors selling local delicacies such as snails and sheep's head soup. Toward the south of the medina are the remains of what was once the palace of the Saadian sultan, Ahmad al-Mansur. Built between 1578 and 1603, the El Badi Palace is a fascinating example of Moorish architecture that once boasted 360 rooms adorned with Italian marble and gold ornaments and a vast courtyard with sunken gardens separated by pools. Elsewhere are important – and beautiful – mosques, shrines and madrasas (Qur'anic schools) such as the stunning decorated archways and courtyards of Ben Youssef Madrasa, which can trace its history back to the 14th century.

Just outside the medina is another of Marrakech's treasures, the Menara gardens, which also date back to the 12th century and are laid out around an elegant pavilion with the Atlas mountains forming a stately backdrop. Elsewhere, the city has more modern delights including the Marrakech Museum that occupies the Grand Menebhi Palace. Built in the 19th century it now displays great works of Moroccan art, old and new, as well as cultural artifacts.

A dazzling city filled with distractions, history and culture, Marrakech is eccentric, colorful and bursting with hidden delights.

Main image: *The red brick remains of the El Badi Palace, which dates to the late 16th century and was once the opulent home of the sultan Ahmad al-Mansur.*

Inset: *The minaret of the Koutoubia mosque, which towers over the Djemaa el Fna marketplace, dates back to the 12th century.*

METEORA MONASTERIES

Throughout history there have been examples of monastic orders devoted to the ideals of peace, solitude and a life led apart from the rest of the world. Few places illustrate their ethos more dramatically than the monasteries of Meteora. Towering up to 615 meters (2,000 ft) over the Plains of Thessaly, near the Pindus mountains in central Greece, these monasteries perch on the summits of sheer-sided sandstone pillars formed 60 million years ago by weathering and earthquakes.

Meaning 'suspended in the air,' the first Meteora monastery was founded in the 9th century when a group of monks scaled the giant sandstone pillars, and stayed there. They lived in the caves or cracks in the stone and met only on days of worship to pray together. By the early 12th century this small group of monks had flourished into a monastic state called the skete of 'Stagoi.' (A 'skete' is a community of Christian hermits). It was centered around the small church of Theotokos ('Mother of God'). The first great monastery was constructed between 1356 and 1372 to the plan of Athanasios Koinovitis, a fellow monk who had traveled to the region from Mount Athos. Situated on the summit of Broad Rock and only accessible by ladder, it offered an ideal haven for the hermitic monks.

In the closing years of the 14th century, when Greece was under threat from Turkish raiders, the monks built refuges on the most inaccessible rocks. As the Turkish invasion escalated, an increasing number sought refuge in the peaks of Meteora and by the beginning of the 15th century construction of over 20 new monasteries had been completed. Access to the buildings was intended to be difficult. Each monastery could only be reached with long ladders and new arrivals were hauled up by rope. It is said that the rope was only replaced 'when the Lord let them break.' Access, however, became easier during the 1920s when steps were carved into the rock.

Now only six of the monasteries remain and each has less than ten residents. The largest is The Holy Monastery of Great Meteoron, which was built during the 14th century and stands 615 meters (2,000 ft) above sea level. The church received substantial donations during the 16th century and many of the original features were restored. Today it also acts as a museum for visitors. Only one monastery is inhabited by women: the Holy Monastery of Saint Stephen. It was founded in the 15th century and is the most easily accessible of all the buildings.

When UNESCO placed the Meteora on the World Heritage List, their criteria stated that these building show 'a masterpiece of human creative genius' and 'contain superlative natural phenomena.' Indeed, few places on Earth incorporate the majesty of nature alongside such impressive examples of the ingenuity and determination of humankind.

Main image: *The Meteora monasteries were built from the late 14th century onward and offered safety and peace to the hermitic monks who lived here.*

Inset: *The remaining six monasteries perch atop sheer sandstone pillars close to Greece's Pindus Mountains.*

MILFORD SOUND

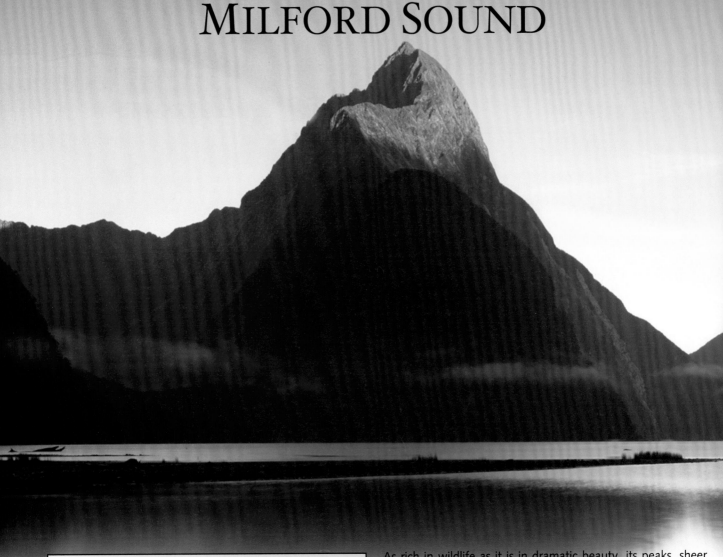

Voted the top tourist destination of 2010 in an international survey, New Zealand's Milford Sound is a singularly picturesque spot in a country that abounds in natural splendor.

As rich in wildlife as it is in dramatic beauty, its peaks, sheer cliffs and lush forests dip into clear waters where dolphins swim alongside the boats of visitors and, occasionally, whales can be seen at play.

Located in the vast Fiordland National Park to the southwest of New Zealand's South Island, Milford Sound runs for 16 kilometers (10 miles) through some of the world's most spectacular Alpine scenery to the open waters of the Tasman Sea. Cradled by steep mountains that rise up to 1,675 meters (5,495 ft) above the water, and from which waterfalls cascade, Maori legend tells that it was created by the god Tu-te-raki-whanoa who split the mountains with his axe. In fact, it is a fjord that was created by a massive glacier during the last ice age. High above sea level, where smaller glaciers once fed into the great slab of ice that craved the fjord, streams now run, to become waterfalls where the main glacier created a sharp drop to the sea below.

The dense forests that cling to the mountainsides of Milford Sound are home to about 700 species of plant life, ranging from the great rimu (*Dacrydium cupressinum*) trees to tree ferns, rare shrubs, flowers and mosses. As might be expected, such a profuse environment is teeming with wildlife, including abundant birdlife, though Milford Sound is most famous for its marine animals, particularly the seals that can be found resting on rocks all year round and the endangered Crested Fiordland Penguin.

Milford Sound was discovered by Europeans in 1812 when Captain John Grono sailed his ship into the fjord's tight opening and named the wonderland he found there for his home, Milford Haven in Wales. Despite being relatively remote – and receiving an average of 6.75 meters (22 ft) of rain each year – word of the fjord's lush beauty quickly spread. By the end of the 19th century, large numbers of people were walking the 53.5 kilometers (33 miles) of what is now recognized as one of the world's best hiking routes, Milford Track, to see its wonders for themselves. Since then, it has become one of the globe's most famous scenic places, attracting around a million visitors per year despite the almost constant rain. Milford Sound offers canoeing and hiking as well as a fantastic underwater observatory from which it is possible to view the rare black corals that grow about 10 meters (30 ft) below the waves.

Main image: *Milford Sound's best known mountain was named Mitre Peak as it resembles a bishop's hat and stands 1,692 meters (5,551 ft) high.*

Inset: *The fjord is well known for its spectacular waterfalls, which are best seen after a heavy rainfall.*

NAZCA LINES

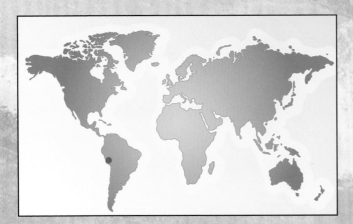

years ago. Seemingly highly civilized, they also manufactured superb ceramics and textiles and built underground aqueducts that are still in use. However, while crafts and building works of this nature are common to many ancient cultures, no one can be sure why the Nazcas made their great geoglyphs. How they made them has proved easier to solve. Archeologists have found wooden stakes driven into the sand at various points in the designs and small teams of researchers have been able to recreate the designs using only simple tools.

Scored into the high desert sands of Peru are 300 giant diagrams that present one of the greatest mysteries of human history. Including geometric designs as well as figures of birds and animals, these 'geoglyphs,' as they are scientifically known, can only be truly appreciated from the air, yet they date back to a time between 200 BC and 700 AD when a now vanished people called the Nazca inhabited the region. No one now knows why they were made, or is even certain who made them, but the great, stylized images lend the landscape an alien strangeness, that is completely unique to the area.

What purpose they served has been more difficult to ascertain and some of the wilder theories have caught the attention of the world in books such as Erich von Däniken's *Chariots of the Gods?* Von Däniken, and others, have suggested that as the geoglyphs could only be seen from above that they served as landing strips for alien spacecraft. The astronomer Phillis Pitluga has put forward the theory that the figures represent the constellations while others have suggested that they may have served other astronomic purposes. Although it is now highly unlikely that we will ever know their true purpose, it is considered more likely that the Nazca Lines were created as simple offerings to the sky gods and may also have been used for rituals.

The Nazca Desert lies about 400 kilometers (250 miles) to the south of the Peruvian capital of Lima close to the coast. It is an arid, barren region of sand, spanning about 500 square kilometers (190 sq miles) covered with a perplexing array of huge drawings ranging from simple lines and spirals to giant plants, lizards, hummingbirds, monkeys, spiders and many other types of fish and animals. Among the geoglyphs are figures that measure up to 200 meters (660 ft) across, but thanks to the dry and stable weather patterns in the area, they have survived for many centuries.

For whatever reason they were made, the lines' mysterious origins and their unearthly beauty have long fascinated humankind. An enduring legacy of a people now gone, they became a UNESCO World Heritage Site in 1994.

Archeologists and historians agree that the lines were in all likelihood made by the Nazca, whose culture died out about 400

Main image: *This huge stylized image of a hummingbird is among the more famous of the Nazca Lines.*

Inset: *Sometimes known as the 'astronaut,' this Nazca drawing, which appears to show a figure wearing some kind of helmet, has been used as evidence that the drawings were connected to space travelers.*

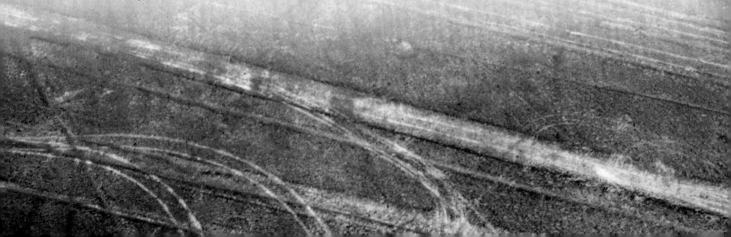

MOUNT NEMRUT

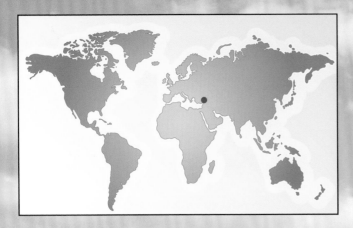

Looking out from the top of Mount Nemrut in Turkey's Taurus Mountains are great statues, over 2,000 years old and shaped to honor one of the region's most celebrated kings, Antiochus I, as well as the gods of Greece and Persia. Now headless, they still present a stunning spectacle, particularly at sunrise, and guard a burial mound that is thought to contain the body of the king himself.

Mount Nemrut (also often called Nemrut Dagi) is located 40 kilometers (25 miles) north of the small town of Kahta in southeastern Turkey, at the heart of what was once the kingdom of Commagene, which existed in the region from about the 3rd century BC until it came under Roman rule in the 1st century AD. The most famous of the Commagene kings was Antiochus I, who ruled between 62 BC and 38 BC, and who claimed descent from the generals of Alexander the Great as well as Persian nobility. During his reign, the nation experienced a 'golden' period and Antiochus fostered a religious tradition which combined the beliefs of Greece and Persia, and also included himself and his family among the pantheon of gods.

The mixture of religions, and the pride Antiochus took in his family tree, is amply demonstrated at his final resting place. At the summit of the 150-meter (7,053-ft) mountain is the tumulus mound beneath which Antiochus is believed to lie. At the foot of his tomb were placed a number of statues, some up to 9 meters (30 ft) high, which include not only a grand representation of himself, but carvings that combined aspects from the Greek and Persian deities (a tradition which was started by Alexander the Great). Thus the Greek Hercules is

identified with the Persian Vahagn, Zeus with Aramazd – the father of the gods in the ancient Armenian pantheon – and so forth. The statues also include two lions and a pair of eagles, while the reliefs on the remains of a carved frieze show the king's Macedonian and Persian ancestors. The seated statues were set in a line on terraces to each of the four sides of the tumulus, facing away, while on the eastern side is an altar. Close by are the tombs of several of Antiochus's successors.

At some point in history the statues were decapitated. While the bodies still sit upright and dignified, the heads were scattered on the ground and the tomb forgotten until discovered by a German named Charles Sester in 1881. Today, Mount Nemrut attracts thousands of visitors each year and is a UNESCO World Heritage Site.

Main image: *Broken heads and the remains of an altar on the flanks of Turkey's Mount Nemrut. The body of King Antiochus is thought to lay beneath the burial mound.*

Inset: *The great statues of Mount Nemrut depict hybrid Greek and Persian gods as well as King Antiochus himself. No one knows when or why they were decapitated.*

NGORONGORO CRATER

Formed 2.5 million years ago by volcanic activity, Tanzania's Ngorongoro Crater lies at the heart of a conservation area and UNESCO World Heritage Site. Home to early ancestors of the human race and now a magnificent habitat for thousands of animals, the great caldera is as geologically and ecologically fascinating as it is strikingly beautiful.

Surrounded by an unbroken rim that rises up to 610 meters (2,000 ft) above the 260 square kilometers (100 sq miles) of its floor, the Ngorongoro Crater lies to the northeast of Tanzania in the Crater Highlands region. As the name suggests, the area is highly volcanic and was created about 25 million years ago, a time of great shifts in the Earth's tectonic plates that also formed the Great Rift Valley. It is thought that when the Ngorongoro

volcano formed, it lay over a subterranean chamber filled with magma that drained away due to further activity in the Earth's crust, leaving a great cavity. About 2.5 million years ago more explosions, together with the vast weight of the volcano's cone, caused it to collapse into the chamber beneath, leaving only a great crater where a mountain that may have been the equal to Mount Kilimanjaro once stood.

The floor of the crater is now primarily grassland, with two small forested areas, and a seasonal salt lake. It has an almost uninterrupted supply of fresh water from the Munge and Lonyokie rivers, which form swamps that are home to hippopotamus. In fact, the crater has often been called a 'natural wildlife enclosure' and is the home of many species, including the greatest concentration of lions in Africa, as well as leopards, elephants and thousands of ungulates: zebra, wildebeest, eland and gazelle. The shallow waters also attract vast numbers of bright pink flamingo. In total, it is estimated that 25,000 animals live here, though the crater rim exacts a price for its protection. Species with smaller numbers, such as the lions, can suffer from genetic problems caused by inbreeding as new additions to the crater's stock are rare.

As well as providing a sanctuary for today's animals, fossils suggest that the Ngorongoro Crater and its surrounding region was once a cradle for hominid species (descendants of mankind) about three million years ago. Close by is Olduvai Gorge, which is thought to be where the first humans evolved. The region has been populated by farming tribes for at least 3,000 years and was ranged by hunter-gatherers before then.

With its unique human heritage, astonishing ecology and great beauty, the Ngorongoro Crater is now part of a protected area, though thousands arrive each year to take safaris and trek through its natural wonders.

Main image: *The lush plains of the Ngorongoro Crater form a 'natural wildlife enclosure' and are abundant with animals.*

Inset: *In total about 25,000 animals – including zebra and elephants – make their home within the relatively small 260 square kilometer (100 sq miles) bowl of the Ngorongoro Crater.*

NIAGARA FALLS

Spanning the border between Canada and the United States on the Niagara River about 27 kilometers (17 miles) from the city of Buffalo are the mighty Niagara Falls. Made up of three sections – Horseshoe Falls on the Canadian side with American Falls and the smaller Bridal Veil over the US border – the great cascades are one of nature's most awe-inspiring sights. In high flow, over 168,000 cubic meters (6 million cu ft) of water cascade over the rim into the basin below each minute, raising great clouds of mist and making a constant deep roar.

The falls were formed at the end of the last ice age – a mere 10,000 years ago – when torrents of water from melting glaciers formed the Great Lakes and the Niagara River. Gradually, the torrential river eroded away the softer rock at the base of the Niagara Escarpment and the second largest waterfall in the world (the largest being Victoria Falls in Zimbabwe) was

formed. In fact, when newly created the falls were located about 11 kilometers (7 miles) downstream, but the constant erosion of the rim has caused them to retreat.

The name 'Niagara' is derived from the Iroquois Indian word *Onguiaahra* which means 'the strait.' The earliest recorded European account of the deluge dates back to 1604 when it was discovered by the French explorer Samuel de Champlain. Over the years, tales of Niagara's majesty and terrifying beauty filtered back to Europe and interest in the site grew. By the 18th century, thousands flocked to see the falls first hand; even royalty crossed the oceans for a chance to witness

their awesome power: Napoleon Bonaparte's brother Jérome, the King of Westphalia, brought his new bride to the falls in the early 19th century. The number of tourists increased again after the American Civil War when the New York Central Railroad, advertised Niagara Falls as 'an ideal honeymoon destination'. They have also witnessed numerous daredevils making death-defying leaps. The first person to plunge over the rim in a barrel was 63-year-old schoolteacher Annie Taylor, in 1901, and others have followed her example despite the fact that such stunts are illegal on both sides of the border.

As with many of the world's most spectacular natural wonders, conservation has become an important issue in recent times and great efforts have been made to slow the ongoing erosion process. In June 1969, for example, the Niagara River was rerouted for several months so that the American Falls could be strengthened and repaired. Today, Niagara Falls welcome over 20 million visitors every year. The crashing torrents of water are renowned worldwide as one of Earth's greatest spectacles, and they also remain a popular tourist destination.

Main image: *A tourist boat navigates into the mists at the base of the Horseshoe Falls.*

Inset: *The view across Niagara Falls. Each minute – at times of the highest flow – over 168,000 cubic meters (6 million cu ft) plunge over the edge.*

NORTHERN LIGHTS

Dance of the Spirits to the Cree tribe, while in Norse mythology the lights are said to be caused by the glowing armor of the *valkyrie* female warriors who fetch the dead from battlefields and bring them to Valhalla.

Nevertheless, the lights are, of course, a purely natural phenomenon and one that is still not fully understood. They occur about 80 kilometers (50 miles) or more above the Earth's surface and are caused by solar 'winds' of electrons and ions given off during solar activity streaming through space and interacting with Earth's magnetic fields and atmospheric gases. Higher in the atmosphere, the light given off is red, while interactions at lower altitudes are green, blue or pale purple. While the Earth experiences solar winds constantly, it is only the most intense activity that is visible to the naked eye, which means that the visitors to high northern latitudes hoping to view Northern Lights for themselves must often wait weeks during the coldest months of the year – the solar wind speed tends to be greatest between early September and early March.

However long they have waited, few visitors are ever disappointed by the display. Although the process that causes the effect may be happening far above, it often seems as if the light displays are just beyond reach. Shining curtains weave across the sky and sometimes streams and whirls of light streak through the atmosphere at higher speeds. At other times, great glimmering clouds seem not to move or curling swirls race across the sky then stop, disappear, then reappear again. Great spears jab toward the Earth. Watching this awe-inspiring show is a spellbinding, moving experience and it is easy to understand why earlier people believed the lights to be caused by spirits or supernatural beings: the Northern Lights do seem as if they have a life of their own.

D ecorating the far northern night skies with ribbons, circles, curtains and spears of ethereal light, the Northern Lights – or the *aurora borealis* as the effect is scientifically known – are one of nature's most astonishing sights. Many who have seen them describe the experience as being almost mystical and it is little wonder that this strange, silent display has given rise to numerous myths and legends.

Usually seen only in the highest latitudes, and most commonly within the Arctic Circle, the *aurora borealis* is named for Aurora, the Roman goddess of the dawn, and the Greek for 'north wind': *boreas*. The fantastic dancing green, and sometimes blue, purple or red, lights have inspired many cultures to ascribe the effect's origin to gods or spirits. In North America, for instance, the Northern Lights are known as the

Opposite page: *A display of aurora borealis lights over the Takeetna Mountains in Alaska. The color of the effects gives an indication of the height at which solar particles are interacting with the Earth's magnetic field.*

Left: *The Northern Lights appear in many forms, from ribbons and spears to spiraling curtains of light. All are spellbindingly beautiful.*

Following pages: *A green aurora seen near the village of Clyde, Alberta, Canada on August 20, 2009.*

OLD FAITHFUL

The world's most famous geyser is not one of the most impressive found on the planet, though it is certainly impressive enough to instill a sense of awe in anyone watching it erupt. It is, however, one of the most predictable. Every hour to an hour and a half – depending on the length of the previous eruption – and for up to five minutes at a time, it expels 14,000 to 32,000 liters (3,700 to 8,400 gallons) of boiling water in a great jet that can reach a height of 55 meters (184 ft). Although the eruptions of close-by Steamboat Geyser are higher, reaching 90 meters (300 ft) on occasion, the fact that Old Faithful's are as frequent as they are grand has made it a favorite for tourists for many years and spread the geyser's fame far and wide.

Located in Yellowstone Park, Wyoming – home to about half of the world's geysers – Old Faithful's eruptions are caused by volcanic activity in the area. The process involves water filtering through the ground and meeting hot volcanic rock at a depth of about 2,000 meters (6,600 ft). This causes the water to boil, creating pressure in much the same way as a steam engine and blasting the water from a surface vent. Old Faithful is known as a 'cone geyser' due to the minerals that have created a volcanic-looking cone around its oval vent.

Old Faithful was first reported to have been witnessed by members of the Washburn-Langford-Doane Expedition in 1870. One of the party leaders – Nathaniel Langford – described the reaction of the party on first seeing the geyser erupt, writing in his journal, 'Judge, then, what must have been our astonishment, as we entered the basin at mid-afternoon of our second day's travel, to see in the clear sunlight, at no great distance, an immense volume of clear, sparkling water projected into the air to the height of one hundred and twenty-five feet. "Geysers! geysers!" exclaimed one of our company, and, spurring our jaded horses, we soon gathered around this wonderful phenomenon.' The spectacular geyser was dubbed 'Old Faithful' by Henry D. Washburn for the regularity of its eruptions and the expedition made detailed notes of its appearance and properties.

Later, stories of the wonders the expedition had found – including Old Faithful – appeared in the press. One member of the party, Cornelius Hedges, recommended conserving the region and within two years it was set aside as Yellowstone National Park, the world's first national park, by President Ulysses S. Grant.

Main image: *While it is not the tallest of Yellowstone National Park's geysers, Old Faithful's eruptions are remarkably predictable, taking place every 60 to 90 minutes.*

Inset: *The geyser is at the heart of the United States' first National Park, a superb wilderness area of great natural beauty that is home to many animals, including bison.*

ORESUND BRIDGE

Spanning a distance of 7,845 meters (25,738 ft) the Oresund Bridge is the longest combined road and rail bridge in Europe, and includes the longest cable-stayed span in the world as part of its length. It stretches between Sweden's third largest city, Malmo, and an artificial island in the Oresund Strait, where traffic descends into a tunnel that emerges close to Denmark's capital, Copenhagen. An incredible feat of construction and a testament to the combined engineering skills of the two countries, for many Scandinavians the Oresund Bridge symbolizes the great possibilities of collaboration between nations.

Designed by Dissing+Weitling, a Danish architectural company, the Oresund Bridge carries two rail tracks and a four-lane highway across the Oresund Strait that separates Denmark from Sweden. Built between 1995 and 1999, it is a 'girder and cable-stayed' bridge with most of its weight supported from beneath by concrete piers, but with a central span that is the longest cable-stayed section of bridge ever built, measuring 490 meters (1,608 ft). The towers to which cables are attached are 204 meters (669 ft) high and give the Oresund Bridge the look of a suspension bridge though, in fact, the engineering principles between the two types are quite different. In a suspension bridge, the cable which stretches from end to end bears the weight of the bridge, while in a cable-stayed structure the towers to which the cables are anchored take the greatest load. As well as giving the bridge a distinctive appearance the cable-stayed section also allows shipping to pass beneath, though most vessels prefer to bypass the bridge altogether, which is made possible by the fact that the final stretch of the Oresund Strait crossing is a tunnel. (The Drogden Tunnel also ensures that air traffic from Copenhagen Airport is unimpeded by the presence of a bridge.) Where the bridge becomes a tunnel is a 4-kilometer (2.5-mile) long artificial island dubbed Peberholm Island, which was constructed mainly from earth and rock excavated during the building of the bridge.

A great source of national pride to both the Swedish and Danes, the completion of the bridge, on August 14, 1999, was marked with a royal meeting at its center. The route across the Oresund Strait was officially opened to traffic – again with royals of both nations in attendance – on June 12, 2000. Since then it has received some criticism for the high prices charged for tolls, though an average 12,000 vehicles and 50,000 people now cross it each day with the number rising annually.

Main image: *The Oresund Bridge stretches almost 8 kilometers (5 miles) across the Oresund Strait, which separates Denmark and Sweden.*

Inset: *The bridge features a distinctive span that is supported by cables, allowing vessels to pass beneath it.*

PALM ISLANDS

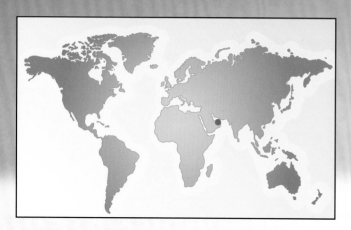

In June 2001, construction work began on one of the most audacious projects in human history – the building of three entirely new islands in the waters of the Persian Gulf, off the coast of Dubai. Each boasts all the trappings of a luxury lifestyle, from opulent hotels and beach side villas, to marinas, spas, high end shopping malls and theme parks. Named Palm Jumeirah, Palm Jebel Ali and Palm Deira, the islands are formed in the shape of palm trees and surrounded by a breakwater crescent. While each island represents a truly monumental undertaking, the last to be completed – Palm Deira – will have a surface area larger than New York's Manhattan Island when finished.

The first, and smallest, of the palm islands is Palm Jumeirah, the construction of which helped pioneer the techniques that would later be used for its larger neighbors. Encircled and protected by 6.3 million tonnes (7 million tons) of rock on the outer edge of its 11-kilometer (7-mile) breakwater island, the palm itself was formed by pouring almost 94 million cubic meters (3.5 billion cu ft) of sand onto the seabed from dredger ships. Gaps in the breakwater allow the movement of water around the island and it has been designed to encourage the

formation of natural reefs as well as to attract other forms of marine life.

Measuring just over 5 kilometres by 5 kilometers (3 x 3 miles) the trunk and fronds of this great palm shape are paved with roads and connected to the mainland by a 300-meter (990-ft) bridge. Along the newly created beachfront are villas, apartment buildings and upscale resort-hotels such as The Palm Atlantis, which features an aquapark and pools where guests can swim with dolphins. The first tenants moved to Palm Jumeirah during April 2009, and the island's homeowners include a number of international celebrities.

Palm Jebel Ali is 50 per cent larger than Palm Jumeirah. When complete, it is expected to be home to some 250,000 people. Construction began in October 2002 and the island will also boast four major theme parks – the first of which is planned to open in 2012 – as well as various other entertainment destinations.

The largest of the three islands, Palm Deira, was begun in 2004 and has no confirmed completion date. However, it will eventually dwarf its smaller sisters at eight times the size of Jumeirah and five times as large as Jebel Ali.

Proclaimed the 'Eighth Wonder of the World' by Nakheel, the construction company responsible for the islands, the three 'Palms' are, indeed, a bold enterprise. Although problems have been experienced during the building work – not least the global credit crunch that began in 2008 – along with the Dubai Waterfront, also being developed by Nakheel, they are part of the greatest reclamation project the world has ever seen.

Main image: *Palm Jumeirah during construction work in 2004. Around the edge of the encircling crescent, rocks prevent the sand from being washed away.*

Inset: *Fireworks are seen during the grand opening of Atlantis, The Palm in Dubai. The resort was the first to open on Palm Jumeirah island.*

PANAMA CANAL

Crossing 82 kilometers (51 miles) of a narrow strip of land between North and South America, and connecting two of the world's great oceans, the Panama Canal is undoubtedly one of the biggest – and costliest – engineering projects ever undertaken. Officially opened on August 15, 1914, with the passage of SS *Ancon*, the first ship to pass through it, the price tag on the canal was the equivalent of an extraordinary $639,000,000. It also cost the lives of more than 30,000 workers, who died during construction.

The idea of creating a channel between the Atlantic and Pacific oceans is almost as old as the European discovery of the Americas. In order to reach the West Coast of North America, and travel onward to Asian ports, ships were forced to sail the infamously perilous passage around Cape Horn at the southern tip of the continent. Creating a shipping channel in the relatively narrow strip of land between the two American continents offered an ideal solution. As early as 1534, Charles V of Spain commissioned a study to discover whether such a route might be possible, while the first detailed plans for a canal were produced in the late 18th century by a Spanish naval officer, an Italian named Alessandro Malaspina.

The first serious effort was made by the French, with permission from the Colombian government, which controlled the territory at the time. Work began on a seawater-level canal on January 1, 1880, but almost immediately ran into problems. Engineers had not taken the trouble to study the land properly and diseases such as malaria and yellow fever quickly spread among the workers. In 1893, having achieved some progress at the cost of over 20,000 lives, the French abandoned the project.

Work began anew on May 4, 1904. The United States government paid $40 million to the French for their construction equipment and to cover the work that had already taken place. Eventually, the US adopted a plan that

would include locks and dams rather than the sea-level channel the French had attempted. This time workers were supplied with decent housing and great efforts were made to combat the diseases that had plagued the French attempt. Even so, almost 6,000 workers died before the canal was completed in 1914.

Including artificial lakes and three series of locks along its length, the Panama Canal is now one of the world's great waterways, cutting almost 12,900 kilometers (8,000 miles) from the journey between New York and San Francisco than would be necessary if a ship rounded Cape Horn. About 15,000 vessels per year make the eight to ten hour voyage through it – paying an average of $54,000 in toll fees.

Main image: *A ship makes its way beneath the Bridge of the Americas, which allows road traffic to cross the Panama Canal close to its Pacific entrance.*

Inset: *Container ships pass through Gatun Locks, which help raise vessels 26 meters (85 ft) above sea level as they navigate through the canal.*

PERITO MORENO GLACIER

The Perito Moreno Glacier is one of Argentina's most impressive sights. With stunning Andean peaks as a backdrop and sunlight making its depths glow a vivid blue, the glacier is not only beautiful but also periodically ruptures where its leading edge meets the chill waters of Lago Argentino (Lake Argentino), providing an awe-inspiring spectacle that cannot be seen anywhere else.

Located in the Los Glaciares National Park (a UNESCO World Heritage Site), in the Santa Cruz Province of Argentine Patagonia, the Perito Moreno Glacier is not the largest of the 48 glaciers that extend from the remains of the Southern Patagonian Ice Field (which once lay over the whole of southern Chile until about the end of the last ice age about 10,000 years ago). Nevertheless, it is easily the most unusual and striking, and the glacier that most visitors to the national park flock to see. About 30 kilometers (19 miles) long, the glacier's surface area is roughly 250 square kilometers (97 sq miles) and it is 5 kilometers (3 miles) wide at its leading edge, which rises to an average height of 74 meters (240 ft) above Lago Argentino. Unusually, it is one of the very few glaciers in the park that is not retreating and, occasionally, it even advances. It is at these times that the great rupture occurs.

Infrequently – sometimes the ruptures are only a year apart, sometimes they are separated by a decade – the glacier advances across the lake to form a natural dam that blocks the flow of water. On the side of the lake that is fed by the Brazo Rico, the water rises up to 30 meters (100 ft), creating an enormous amount of pressure. In trying to break through the barrier, the

lake water filters beneath the glacial ice where it meets the ground. Over a few days, a tunnel is created, weakening the wall of ice so that eventually it cracks and falls apart under the pressure of the water behind it. With a deafening crash, the glacier breaks apart in a spectacular fashion; an event that is watched by up to 20,000 tourists, many of whom make the trip especially to witness the phenomenon.

Even at times when the Perito Moreno Glacier is not rupturing it can still provide dramatic moments: more frequently, large chunks of ice fall from its edge into the water. Due to the spectacles that the glacier provides, as well as the beauty of the surrounding area, which abounds with rare species of flora and fauna, the site is one of Argentina's most visited places and attracts many thousands of trekkers and sightseers each year.

Main image: *Tourists look out over the leading edge of the Perito Moreno Glacier where it flows into the waters of Lago Argentino. Floating in the lake are great chunks of ice that have broken away from the glacier.*

Inset: *A massive chunk of ice breaks off the Perito Moreno Glacier wall creating a large splash and wave during a process known as 'calving.'*

PETRA

The city of Petra is one of the world's most fascinating archeological sites and one of the most visually stunning. Reached only by a narrow gorge, it was once a major hub on the trade routes of the ancient world and over a period of roughly 2,000 years its fabulous architecture developed to

Opposite page: *One of Petra's most famous structures, the Treasury, or El-Khazneh, is a Classical building carved into the pink sandstone rock.*

Below: *The tombs of Petra were built in a range of styles over the centuries and include structures of early Nabataean design as well as those influenced by Greek, Egyptian and Syrian architecture.*

incorporate the styles and traditions of many of the people who passed through the city. Its magnificent buildings – including great churches, tombs, monuments, sacrificial altars and galleries – are carved from the red rock at the side of a valley on Jordan's Mount Hor and are on a scale that dwarf the human visitor.

Located on a providential site at what came to be a crossroads between Arabia, Egypt and Syria-Phoenicia, early settlers of the city were likely to have been attracted by the sheer rocks and the entrance gorge, which would have helped to defend the inhabitants from attackers, as well as a stream that provided water in this arid area. In fact, historians and archeologists believe that Petra was already well established by the time that it was first mentioned in Egyptian military records dating to about 1,500 BC.

By about the 6th century BC the city was controlled by a people known as the Nabataeans, traders who left no written records but who are believed to have embraced many of the customs of the cultures their commerce brought them in touch with. It was the Nabataeans who ensured that Petra blossomed. A desert tribe, they were skilled at collecting and preserving stores of water, and at Petra they created a system of conduits, dams and reservoirs that allowed them to accumulate the waters of occasional floods, providing a supply through even lengthy periods of drought. By the beginning of the 1st century BC, Petra was firmly established as a desert oasis and a stopping place for caravans and merchants.

As the centuries passed the city prospered and its citizens used their wealth to create dizzying building works hewn from the rocks of their home. Numerous styles can be seen to have predominated during different periods, with the simple Nabataean approach of earlier parts giving way to Egyptian, Greek and Roman styles. By the end of the 4th century AD, however, the city's fortunes had waned as traders increasingly favored sea travel. In 383, Petra was struck by an earthquake that damaged its vital water system and the city was gradually abandoned.

Rediscovered by Europeans in 1812, Petra has since become a major tourist destination. Designated a UNESCO World Heritage Site in 1985 and one of the New Seven Wonders of the World in 2007, most famous among its structures today are the Classical designs of some of its largest works. The symmetrical pediments and columns of the Treasury building (known as El-Khazneh locally), for example, have appeared in numerous movies, including *Indiana Jones and the Last Crusade*.

PETRONAS TWIN TOWERS

The world's tallest buildings from their completion in 1998 until Taipei 101 was built in 2004, the Petronas Twin Towers soar above the city of Kuala Lumpur, Malaysia. Rising to

Opposite page: *At night, the Petronas Towers are lit by floodlights, shining and soaring over Kuala Lumpur's skyline.*

Below: *At the foot of the Petronas Towers is KLCC park, which is often used by residents and boasts lakes and fountains, sculpture and children's wading pools as well as a large shopping mall.*

a height of 451.9 meters (1,482 ft) at the tip of their crowning pinnacles, and joined by a skybridge 170 meters (558 ft) above the ground, they are a graceful, yet imposing, feature of the city's skyline and among the world's most easily recognized buildings.

The design of the two towers was spearheaded by the architects César Pelli and Djay Cerico of Argentina. Pelli, who the American Institute of Architects recognizes as one of the ten most influential living American architects, based the design on Islamic artwork as well as the characteristics of the country. He later said of the design process, 'I tried to express what I thought were the essences of Malaysia, its richness in culture and its extraordinary vision for the future. The building is rooted in tradition and about Malaysia's aspiration and ambition.'

Constructed atop the world's deepest foundations, which plumb 115 meters (377 ft) into the ground to reach secure bedrock, each tower contains 88 floors constructed with reinforced concrete and served by 29 high speed elevators as well as 765 flights of stairs. The towers' floor template is based on two interlocking squares – a common form in Islamic design – with the inner angles made less stark with a semi-circular design that also adds to the total useable floor space inside. As each tower rises, it is stepped back repeatedly and the highest levels slope gently inward, helping to create a classic 'spire' effect that also recalls the nation's architectural heritage. Both are surmounted by 73.5-meter (241-ft) spires that were based on the minarets common to many mosques. At the 41st and 42nd floors tenants can cross from one building to the other via a double-level enclosed bridge that is designed to move in and out of each tower as it sways. The towers were both clad in 83,500 square meters (898,800 sq ft) of stainless steel and just over 55,000 square meters (592,000 sq ft) of laminated glass, which provide a glittering façade that is illuminated at night.

A combination of exquisite design and state-of-the-art engineering, the Petronas Towers may no longer be the world's tallest, but they are a much beloved part of the cityscape and the pride of the Malaysian people.

PONT DU GARD

A grand, and beautifully designed, aqueduct that forms part of a system which stretches 50 kilometers (31 miles) through southern France, the Pont du Gard is a superb example of Roman architectural and construction techniques that dates back to the mid-1st century AD. Testament to the builders' skill,

it stands virtually intact almost 20 centuries later, still bearing marks and graffiti scored into the stone by those who raised it.

Located in the Gard *département* in central southern France, close by the commune of Remoulins, the Pont du Gard was part of a system that supplied water to the city of Nimes, which, by the middle of the 1st century AD, was a Roman colony called Nemausus. At that time the colony had become home to a population of about 20,000 people, a number that placed a strain on the area's water resources. The response was typically Roman, and typically audacious: the construction of an aqueduct to carry water south from the distant Fontaines d'Eure springs. While the Pont du Gard is rightly famous as its most impressive section, the whole of the aqueduct represents an astonishing achievement. Over its length, channels, pipes and bridges carry water down a smooth gradient, dropping just 12 meters (39 ft) over the span and allowing water to flow under the force of gravity alone. When completed, after 15 years of construction work, the aqueduct delivered so much water to Nemausus that it not only quenched the thirst of

the colony's citizens, but allowed them to build ornamental fountains and spas as well.

The Pont du Gard itself is a striking work of architecture. Built on three levels, each supported by a row of graceful arches, the highest – which carries the water conduit – stretches just over 275 meters (900 ft) across the Gardon River valley at a height of 49 meters (160 ft). The bottom level carries a road. The entire bridge was built without binding any of the blocks together with mortar. Masons meticulously cut each stone to fit snugly against its neighbors and each was raised with a block and tackle to be slipped into place while the unfinished bridge was supported by scaffolding. Evidence of the construction techniques can still be found on the stones of the Pont du Gard as well as marks that served as building instructions to workers.

Although the aqueduct had fallen out of use by the 9th century, the Pont du Gard continued to be used as a bridge up until the 18th century, by which time it had already become a tourist attraction – a fact that led to several restoration works being carried out over the following century. Today, it remains one of the most visited places in the South of France, and it was designated a UNESCO World Heritage Site in 1985.

Main image: *A superb example of Roman architecture and engineering skill, the Pont du Gard spans the Gardon River in the South of France.*

Inset: *The bridge comprises three levels of arches, the lowest of which is a road crossing. The highest contained the channel through which water flowed on its way to Nimes.*

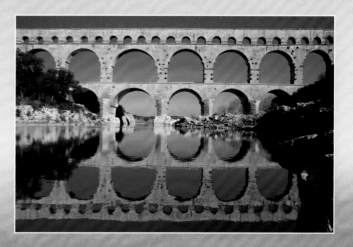

POTALA PALACE

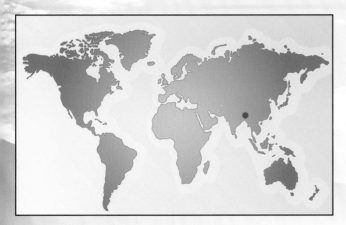

In the city of Lhasa, Tibet, perched on the slopes of Mount Potala, is the imposing Potala Palace. Home to the Dalai Lama until 1959, the palace is an impressively advanced construction and was the world's tallest building for hundreds of years. It is 400 meters (1,300 ft) wide (from east to west), 350 meters (1,150 ft) long (from north to south) and 117 meters (384 ft) tall. The base of each wall averages 5 meters (16 ft) in thickness and copper added to the foundations helps to protect against earthquake damage. Built over 13 stories and situated 300 meters (1,000 ft) above the valley floor, it boasts numerous buildings, over 1,000 rooms, more than 10,000 shrines and in excess of 200,000 statues.

Construction of the Potala Palace began in 1645 after the Great Fifth Dalai Lama, Lozang Gyatso, realized that Mount Potala would be an ideal site for his government, as it was situated between two of Tibet's most eminent monasteries, Drepung and Sera. Although the Dalai Lama moved into the White Palace (*Potrang Karpo*) in 1649, construction was not completed until 1694 – 12 years after his death. The addition of the Red Palace (*Potrang Marpo*) followed between 1690 and 1694.

Apart from the White Palace, which served chiefly as the Dalai Lama's residence and contained secular buildings, such as offices and printing houses, the Potala has a wealth of other buildings within its confines. The cavernous Red Palace is a labyrinth of chapels, halls, galleries and tombs. The Great West Hall of the Red Palace alone boasts four chapels, each dedicated to the Fifth Dalai Lama. Murals cover the walls, each

one illustrating important events in his life. Considered the most holy of all these chapels is The Saint's Chapel, on the northern side of the Great West Hall. Within the chapel walls is a jeweled statue of Avalokiteshvara – the enlightened being said to embody the compassion of all Buddhists. The slightly less well known but equally impressive West Chapel is famed for its five golden *stupas* – huge mound-shaped structures which usually hold important relics. The largest *stupa,* in the center of the chapel, contains the mummified remains of the Fifth Dalai Lama.

The Potala Palace became a UNESCO World Heritage Site in 1994 and since then the Chinese government has done much to preserve the site. The palace has also undergone massive restoration works, using only traditional materials and master craftsmen. Despite restrictions on the number of visitors allowed to enter, this jewel of ancient Tibet attracts over 2,000 people every day.

Main image: *The stunning Potala Palace in Tibet was the residence of the Dalai Lama from the 17th century until the Chinese invasion of 1959.*

Inset: *Richly decorated throughout, the Potala Palace is a complex maze that contains more than 1,000 rooms.*

Following pages: *The Potala Palace, reflected in the lake at the back of the palace.*

PYRAMIDS OF GIZA

Without doubt the world's most famous buildings, the complex of pyramids at Giza includes the Great Pyramid, the last of the Seven Wonders of the Ancient World and a building so enormous that the great cathedrals of Florence, Milan and Rome as well as London's St. Paul's and Westminster Abbey could easily be accommodated within it. Surrounded by desert and shrouded in mystery, the pyramids have captivated the imaginations of billions of people over thousands of years.

Located just outside of Cairo, Egypt's capital city, are three pyramids that – along with the Great Sphinx, smaller tombs and pyramids, monuments, temples and processional ways – comprise the Giza necropolis: a monumental city built to honor the dead. The site is, however, dominated by its largest structures, the Great Pyramid (also known as the Pyramid of Cheops or the Pyramid of Khufu), the slightly smaller Pyramid of Khafre and – smaller again – the Pyramid of Menkaure. Dating back more than 4,500 years, these once held the mummified remains of Egypt's great kings as well as fabulous funerary treasures.

Although it is often thought that slave labor was used to erect the pyramids, evidence suggests that they were built by ordinary Egyptians conscripted for the purpose and working – 100,000 at a time – in three-month shifts. Even for fabulously wealthy Egypt, the cost was crippling and some stories relate that Pharaoh Khufu forced his own daughter into prostitution to help pay for building work that is believed to have taken over 20 years. Finished, the Great Pyramid would have stood 146 meters (479 ft) high – it is now 137 meters (449 ft) due to the fact that its original polished limestone casing has been lost. An almost perfect square at its base with each side measuring 230 meters (756 ft), with a difference of only a few centimeters between its

longest and shortest sides, it is believed that up to 2.3 million blocks were used in its construction. Weighing between 11.5 and 15 tonnes (2.75–16.5 tons) each, these were positioned with incredible precision to within 5/1000ths of an inch.

The smaller two pyramids are almost as impressive: the Pyramid of Khafre is believed to have been 143.5 meters (471 ft) tall when finished while Menkaure's, at 66.5 meters (218 ft) may have been half the size of Khufu's but is still an impressive structure by any standards. In fact, even in this technological age, aspects of the pyramids' construction still baffle scientists. For example, while it is possible to analyze the chemical make-up of the mortar that holds the blocks together, which is harder than the stones themselves, no one has yet been able to fathom how it was made.

A UNESCO World Heritage Site since 1979, the Pyramids of Giza remain one of the planet's most distinctive sights and retain their power to remind visitors of the awesome might of the pharaohs who built them.

Main image: *Although their contents were pillaged long ago, the sheer scale and perfection of the pyramids' construction recalls a rich and technologically advanced culture over which the pharaoh presided as both a king and a god.*

Inset: *Before the pyramid of Khafre is another of Egypt's great treasures: the Great Sphinx, which dates to around 2500 BC.*

PYRAMIDS OF MEROË

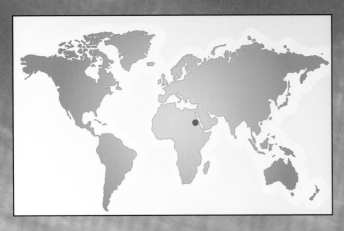

Kush, one of the first civilizations to settle in the fertile lands of the Nile Valley. Although little of the city remains today, this unique site still boasts over 200 Nubian pyramids. Smaller than the world-renowned pyramids of Giza, but presenting a striking sight amid the eerie calm of the desert, the Nubian pyramids of Meroë are as steeped in history as their larger northern neighbors.

Historians believe that the Kushites began moving to Meroë in about 591 BC, and by 300 BC it had become Nubia's capital city. It was at this time that the kings and queens of Kush began to build their burial tombs here. Over the following centuries the city grew in prosperity, enjoying trade with Rome and the rest of Europe. However, by 300 AD, the weakening of its industries and an ongoing

Hidden in the desert sands of Sudan just off the eastern bank of the River Nile, stand the ruins of the once great city of Meroë, the capital city of the ancient kingdom of

struggle against Roman Egypt caused the slow deterioration of the kingdom that led to its eventual collapse. Now, all that remains of this once great empire are the ruined tombs.

Rediscovered in 1821 by French mineralogist Frédéric Cailliaud, the pyramids of Meroë vary in height but are rarely taller than 30 meters (100 ft). Unlike their Egyptian counterparts, the Nubians built their pyramids with smaller foundations, most often having a maximum width of 8 meters (26 ft). This resulted in tall, narrow constructions with an incline of approximately 70 degrees, giving the Nubian pyramids a distinct appearance. Traditionally each entrance was adorned by an Egyptian-style offering temple at the base though very few of these have withstood the ravages of time.

Like their Egyptian neighbors, the kings and queens of Kush were buried with valuable and useful artifacts to take with them into the afterlife. Early excavations of the tombs unearthed bows, quivers of arrows, furniture, glassware and – in one case – the remains of a cow. Unfortunately, and again like the Egyptian pyramids, these tombs were also raided by treasure hunters, leaving them bare of most of their riches.

However, in 1834, an excavation led by Guiseppe Ferlini found a small amount of ancient jewelry, which is now housed in museums in Berlin and Munich.

Although an ongoing civil war in Sudan has made further archeological investigations difficult, much is being done to restore the site. Several pyramids have been restored completely and several more buildings excavated, including the Lion Temple, which contains many well preserved wall paintings.

Main image: *Dating to between 300 BC and 300 AD, the burial pyramids of Meroë are now in various stages of ruin, but their unexpected symmetry in the midst of desert sands is a powerful reminder of the civilization that built them.*

Inset: *Smaller and steeper-sided than the pyramids of Egypt, Meroë's tombs are now Sudan's most popular tourist attraction.*

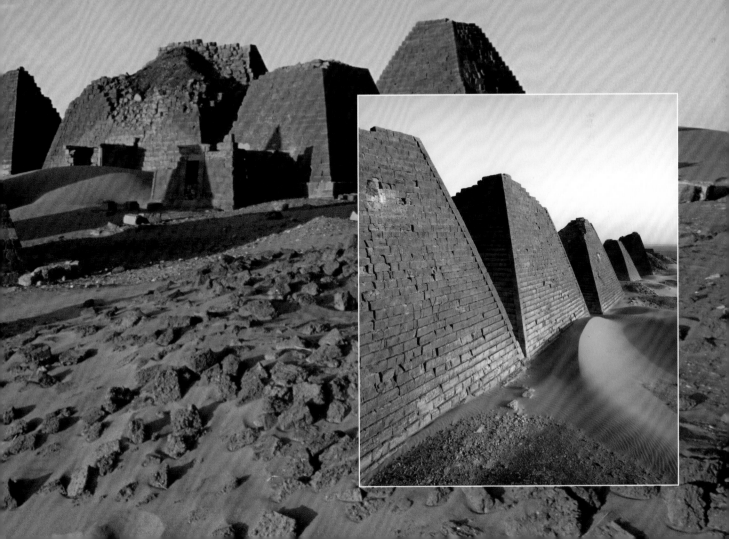

REDWOOD NATIONAL AND STATE PARKS

majestically towering giant redwoods are the most famous of species here, among the park's other inhabitants are black bears, elk and bald eagles, while off the rocky shoreline dolphins and whales can sometimes be seen breaking the water.

Now comprising a total area of 534 square kilometers (206 sq miles) along California's northern coast, the Redwood National and State Parks are both a UNESCO World Heritage and Biosphere site. Including grasslands and 60 kilometers (37 miles) of coast within their boundaries, parts of today's parks have been protected since the 1920s. Earlier in the region's history – roughly 3,000 years ago – numerous Native-American tribes lived here, dwelling in homes built from planks cut from fallen redwoods. Many of their descendants can still be found in the area. In 1850, gold was discovered in the region, sparking a rush that brought tens of thousands of new people to the area. Not all struck it rich and many turned to logging to earn a living. At the time, San Francisco was growing rapidly. There was a voracious appetite for wood and the redwood forests

Home to many of the world's tallest trees, some of which are over 2,000 years old, as well as other rare, and threatened, plants and animals, the Redwood National Park is a rich and spectacularly beautiful ecosystem. While the

appeared to offer an inexhaustible supply. By the early 20th century, the forests had been much diminished and the Save-the-Redwoods League was created and successfully lobbied for preserves to be set aside. Nevertheless, logging proceeded elsewhere and by the 1960s about 90 percent of the region's redwood forest had disappeared. In 1968, however, Redwood National Park was created and more land has been periodically added to the park in the years since.

The park is, of course, dominated by the great trees that give it its name. Otherwise known as *Sequoia sempervirens*, coast redwood or California redwood, the trees are unique to the region and can reach heights of up to about 115 meters (377 ft). Living up to 2,200 years, the largest can measure 8 meters (26 ft) in diameter at the base of their trunk. Other species of tree, however, are also common throughout the park – notably the Douglas fir – while at lower levels shrubs such as the Californian rhododendron and azalea add splashes of color to the scenery. The different ecosystems – woodland, prairie, river, prairie and coast – also support numerous species of animal, some of which, such as the bald eagle, northern spotted owl and Steller's sea lion, are endangered. High above the forest floor live northern flying squirrels while mountain lions, bobcats, river otter, beaver and black-tailed deer also make the park their home.

Today, the Redwood National and State Parks are strictly managed by the National Park Service and the Californian Department of Parks and Recreation, with staff working to ensure that the area remains pristine. Apart from a single youth hostel, no hotels or resorts are allowed in the area, though the parks are popular with hikers and campers.

Main image: *A shroud of fog blankets a forest in Redwood National Park.*

Inset: *Sword ferns grow at the base of old redwood trees. The parks' ecosystems support a great variety of rare flora and fauna.*

MOUNT RUSHMORE

The vast carvings were the brainchild of Doane Robinson, a South Dakota state historian who hoped that the creation of a great sculpture in the state's Black Hills would attract tourists to the area. In August 1924, Robinson presented his idea to sculptor Gutzon Borglum who, at that time, was working on the great bas-relief of Confederate leaders on the side of Stone Mountain in Georgia. Borglum visited Robinson and accepted the commission. During a second visit, Mount Rushmore was chosen as the most promising site for the carvings.

By March 3, 1925, Congress had approved the creation of

Gazing down from the upper slopes of Mount Rushmore in South Dakota's Black Hills are the monumental faces of four of the United States' greatest presidents – George Washington, Thomas Jefferson, Abraham Lincoln and Theodore Roosevelt. Eighteen meters (60 ft) tall, and cut directly into the granite cliffs, these sculptures are known to millions around the world.

the site and Borglum worked on finalizing his plans for the sculptures. Under orders from President Calvin Coolidge to include two Republicans and a Democrat alongside George Washington, Borglum selected Jefferson, Lincoln and Roosevelt for their contributions to expanding, preserving and unifying the nation during its first century and a half of independent history. Originally, as can be seen from an early model, Borglum hoped to sculpt each figure to the waist, but budgetary restraints caused this ambition to be scaled back.

On August 10, 1927, President Coolidge presented Borglum with a set of drill bits and the first drilling commenced amid much ceremony. Serious work began on October 4, with 400 workers blasting rock from the cliffs using dynamite (90 per cent of the actual carving was done using explosives). First to be completed was the head of Washington, which was dedicated on July 4, 1934. Next was Jefferson. Originally his face was planned to appear on Washington's right, but after 18 months of work the sculpture was destroyed after the rock there was found to be inappropriate and fresh work began to Washington's left. The completed sculpture was dedicated by President Franklin D. Roosevelt on August 30, 1936. Lincoln's sculpture was dedicated on September 17, 1937 and Roosevelt's two years later, on July 2, 1939.

Finishing work – including the creation of a 'Sculptor's Studio' – continued until October 1941, for the last seven months of which the project came under the direction of Lincoln Borglum, the sculptor's son. Gutzon Borglum had died in March of that year.

Placed on the National Register of Historic Places in 1966, Mount Rushmore is now visited by about two million people each year, fulfilling Doane Robinson's dream of creating a popular tourist attraction. Due in part to the grandeur of the setting and the scale of the carvings, and in part to the role that each of the presidents played in the early years of American history, the sculptures, and Mount Rushmore itself, have become an international symbol of American freedom and ambition.

Main image: *The great presidential heads of Mount Rushmore are one of the world's most famous sights. From left to right: George Washington, Thomas Jefferson, Theodore Roosevelt and Abraham Lincoln.*

Inset: *Giving a sense of scale, a National Park worker checks Lincoln's nose for cracks.*

SACRED MOSQUE OF MECCA

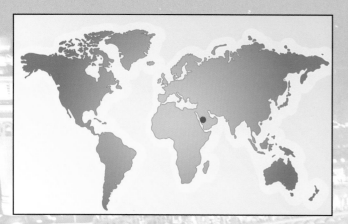

Also known as Al-Masjid al-Haram, the Haram and the Grand Mosque, the Sacred Mosque of Mecca is the largest mosque in the world and surrounds the *Kaaba* – the most sacred site in the Islamic religion, and the place toward which all Muslims turn to offer their prayers. A vast space, steeped in holiness and history, the Sacred Mosque is one of the world's most revered and important religious sites.

Located in the Mecca, in Saudi Arabia, the Sacred Mosque and its environs (which include outdoor praying areas) cover an area of almost 4,000 square kilometers (1,000 acres). The space is sufficient to contain four million Muslims during the time of the *Hajj*, a pilgrimage that takes place annually from the 8th to 12th days of the final month of the Islamic year. While a mosque has existed here since the 7th century, when the city was home to the Prophet Muhammad, very little of the older buildings remain. The mosque has been damaged and destroyed on numerous occasions by floods and fire, and the oldest parts of the structure now date back to the late 16th century when it was renovated under Sultan Selim II. Today's Sacred Mosque is largely the result of much more recent renovations that have been underway since the 1980s, though it remains an excellent example of Islamic architecture, featuring arched galleries, minarets and domes inscribed with passages from the Koran.

At the heart of the Sacred Mosque is the *Kaaba*, a cube-like structure that measures 13.1 meters (43 ft) high with the sides being 11.03 meters (36 ft) by 12.86 meters (42 ft). Its four corners are approximately aligned to the four points of the compass. Now concealed behind a curtain of black and gold, the *Kaaba* is believed by Muslims to have been built by Abraham (Ibrahim) and his son Ishmael on the foundations of a building that was raised by Adam soon after the world was created. Restored under Muhammad after a flood, the walls of the *Kaaba* also contain, at the eastern corner, the Black Stone, a relic that is said to have tumbled from Heaven in order to show Adam and Eve where to build their altar to God and which was set in position by the prophet himself when renovation work had finished. Few, now, are allowed inside the *Kaaba*, but its perfumed interior is clad with marble, which has been inlaid with verses from the Koran, from the floor to about halfway to the ceiling. The top half of the interior walls are draped with green fabric, again bearing Koranic passages.

As the spiritual center of Islam, it is required that any able Muslim must make the *Hajj* pilgrimage to Mecca at least once in their lifetime and for centuries the Sacred Mosque has welcomed millions of visitors each year. All *Hajj* pilgrims, as well as those of the *Umrah* (lesser pilgrimage) are required to walk around the *Kaaba* seven times in a counterclockwise direction. Many who are able also stop to kiss the Black Stone seven times, a tradition begun by the prophet.

Opposite page: *The Sacred Mosque today is a vast complex with the* Kaaba *as its focal point. Each year many millions of pilgrims journey here and some four million can pray within the mosque's confines at any one time.*

Below: *The most sacred site in Islam, all Muslims pray in the direction of the* Kaaba.

SAHARA DESERT

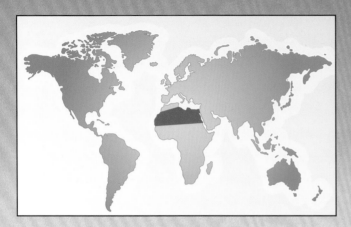

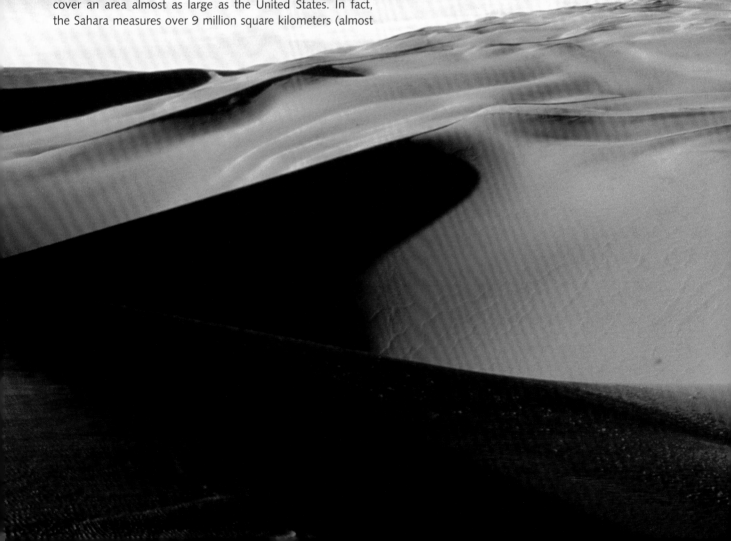

Erily beautiful, with heat hazes shimmering across far horizons and punctuated by island oases, the Sahara is an ocean of wind-sculpted dunes. Here, seemingly endless sands cover an area almost as large as the United States. In fact, the Sahara measures over 9 million square kilometers (almost 3.5 million square miles), and covers most of Northern Africa – from the Atlas Mountains to the north and the Niger River to the south, the Red Sea to the east and the Atlantic Ocean to the west. Yet within this barren landscape are areas of truly unique beauty and life that can be found nowhere else on the planet.

With its name deriving from the Arabic *sahra*, meaning 'desert', the Sahara is thought to have a history spanning almost three million years. The climate has by no means remained constant during this time and, over the last hundred thousand years, has swung between drenched and dry and back again. At the end of the last ice age, between 8,000 and 6,000 BC, the Sahara was much larger than it is today, but increased rainfall caused by melting glaciers pushed back its boundaries. As the glaciers slowly disappeared, less rain fell and the sun scorched the lands of the northern Sahara while the southern tip of the desert was still regularly visited by monsoons, slowing the desertification process. The Sahara achieved its current dimensions by about 3400 BC, when the Earth's changing climate pushed the rains further south. Today, the parched wilderness is again as dry as it was 13,000 years ago with the northern, sub-tropical half receiving less than 76 millimeters (3 in) of rain per year and the southern, tropical half getting only slightly more at 127 millimeters (5 in) per year.

The relentless heat and insufficient water mean that only the most resilient, well-adapted, animals can survive in the Sahara. Dromedary camels were one of the first to be domesticated. They can go for long periods without water and their endurance and speed has made them useful to nomadic tribes such as the Tuareg. Animals such as the addax (a large white antelope) and the dorcas gazelle live comfortably in the desert and, again, can go for months without water. The Sahara is also home to vipers, scorpions, lizards, cheetahs and ostriches.

Despite its harsh climate, the Sahara has been inhabited for thousands of years. Many tribes settled on its unwelcoming lands, including Egyptians, Nubians and Greeks, though the oldest-known inhabitants are the Berbers. Evidence of their civilization can be found across the Sahara in the form of ancient rock paintings and tombs. The Berbers are mentioned in many ancient Egyptian and Greek writings and still inhabit the Sahara today.

Main image: *The seemingly endless sands of the Sahara Desert create an incredible vista where sharp-edged dunes slice light and shadow into great curving waves.*

Inset: *Surrounded by date palms and sand dunes, the Oum el Ma Lake, in Libya, is a beautiful example of a Saharan oasis.*

SAINT PETER'S BASILICA

I n the heart of the Vatican City in Rome lies one of the holiest Christian sites in the world, Saint Peter's Basilica. Called 'the greatest of all churches,' the basilica's sublime architecture, unique heritage and the famous artistic contributions of Michelangelo have attracted the Christian faithful through its doors for centuries.

Built on the site of Saint Peter's tomb, and over an original basilica that dates back to the 4th century, work on the present structure began in 1506. Pope Nicholas V, on seeing the dilapidated condition of the original church at the end of the 15th century, ordered it to be rebuilt. However, political upheavals stalled his plans and Pope Nicholas died before any serious work had been undertaken. In 1505, the old basilica was demolished by order of Pope Julius II who held a competition for architects to submit their designs. Although the designs of Donato Bramante won the competition, many other famous architects and artists embellished them as the structure grew over the next 120 years. After passing through the hands of Guiliano da Sangallo, Fra Gioncondo and Raphael, to name but a few, the task of completing the colossal basilica fell to the renowned Michelangelo.

Michelangelo reluctantly agreed to take the position of 'Capomaestro' in January 1547, after Pope Paul III bullied him to do so. He wrote in his journal, 'I undertake this only for the love of God and in honour of the Apostle.' He reviewed the many different plans from all the previous architects and incorporated the best aspects from each design.

He reverted back to the original Greek Cross floor plan designed by Bramante, yet kept Raphael's extended nave. He also designed and oversaw construction of the huge central dome. The dome reaches 137 meters (449 ft) and is the tallest in the world. Unfortunately, Michelangelo died before the dome was completed, but work continued under the watchful eyes of Pope Sixtus, who hired Giancomo della Porta and Domenico Fontana to complete Michelangelo's vision. In 1590, the dome was finished.

Work on the basilica continued when Pope Paul V engaged Carlo Maderno in 1602 to enhance the building. Moderno added a façade with Corinthian columns and statues of Christ with each of his Apostles. Just behind the façade he built a long corridor called a 'narthex' containing five massive doorways, adorned with columns and statues. Finally he added a nave inside the church, adorned with marble, sculptures, gilt and mosaics.

Today, the basilica contains the tombs of 91 popes as well as various European monarchs and Roman remains dating back to the time of the original basilica. With Saint Peter's Piazza stretching before its entrance, a front balcony is occasionally used by the Pope to bless the assembled crowd of pilgrims, many thousands of whom flock to Saint Peter's each year.

Main image: *The great dome and façade of Saint Peter's Basilica viewed from across the Ponte Sant'Angelo, often called the 'bridge of Saint Peter' because it was used by pilgrims making their way to the basilica.*

Inset: *Designed by Michelangelo, the nave of Saint Peter's Basilica was intended to be a soaring space, flooded with light.*

SERENGETI

Most famous, perhaps, for the great herds of animals that cross its grassy plains twice a year, the Serengeti is a vast and endlessly beautiful landscape that also includes rocky outcrops known as *kopjes*, towering volcanoes, forests, rivers and acacia woodlands. Now containing several national parks, two UNESCO World Heritage Sites and two UNESCO World Biospheres, the great vistas of the Serengeti moved Stewart Edward White, one of the first explorers to see the area, to write in 1913, 'We walked for miles over burnt out country... Then I saw the green trees of the river, walked two miles more and found myself in paradise.'

Stretched across roughly 30,000 square kilometers (11,500 sq miles) of northwest Tanzania and southwest

Kenya, over 80 per cent of the Serengeti region is protected and includes the Serengeti National Park, the Ngorongoro Conservation Area, Maswa Game Reserve, the Loliondo, Grumeti and Ikorongo Controlled Areas, as well as the Maasai Mara National Reserve in Kenya. Once ranged by pre-human *Homo habilis*, whose tools can still be found in the Olduvai Gorge, and date back about 2.6 million years, the area became home to the Maasai between the 17th and 18th centuries.

The Serengeti ecosystem is one of the Earth's oldest and is thought to have changed little over the past million years. It supports a great number of species – the rocky *kopjes* alone are home to hundreds of species of plants and smaller mammals that are unique to the region. Larger mammals, such as wildebeest, gazelle, zebra, giraffe and buffalo, inhabit the great grassy plain, and each October and April create one of nature's greatest spectacles: the great migration that is held to be one of the Natural Wonders of the World. The longest overland migration on Earth, it is made up of huge herds – some two million animals in all – traveling hundreds of kilometers across plains and gorges, and braving rivers full of crocodiles in pursuit of the rains and newly lush grazing grounds.

Other mammals found here include the 'Big Five' – lions, leopards, rhinos, elephant and Cape Buffalo, so named because they were they were considered the most dangerous of the species here, and so presented the greatest thrill for big game hunters. Today, the hunting of big game is strictly prohibited, but the area is visited by over 90,000 tourists each year, eager to catch sight of Africa's famous wildlife amid some of the continent's most incredible scenery.

Main image: *Thousands of blue wildebeest ford the Mara River during the twice annual migration across the Serengeti.*

Inset: *Among the Serengeti grasslands, distinctive acacia trees are such a common sight that the tree has become almost a symbol of the African landscape.*

SOLAR ECLIPSE

Acomplete solar eclipse is so rare that most people would count themselves lucky to witness just one within their lifetime. It is a natural phenomenon so spellbinding that some travel the globe in the hope of glimpsing it. For during an eclipse the world goes black and even birds stop singing before, with a blaze of light known as the 'diamond ring effect', the moon passes and the sun re-emerges. For those who experience the sun abruptly 'turned off' in this manner, it is easy to understand how a solar eclipse was considered a bad omen in centuries past when no one had a real understanding of astronomy.

An eclipse happens when the moon passes between the Earth and the sun. It can only occur during a new moon and only when the sun and the moon are in direct alignment. Even then, a total solar eclipse can only be seen from specific points on the Earth's surface because the shadow of the moon, also called its 'umbra' follows a very narrow path across our planet. Each year there are often up to five solar eclipses, but only two will be total.

There are four categories of solar eclipse. The first is a 'total eclipse,' which occurs when the sun is completely hidden behind the moon and only a small corona is visible. The point when the sun is completely hidden is known as a 'totality;' this never continues for longer than 7 minutes 31 seconds, as the moon continues its orbit around the Earth at 1,700 kilometers per hour (1,056 mph) and moves out of position. It is calculated that fewer than ten eclipses in 1,000 years will have a totality lasting longer than seven minutes and the next is not due until June 25, 2150. The second type is called an 'annular eclipse' and is similar to a total eclipse in that the sun and moon are aligned but, because of the elliptical orbits of these two heavenly bodies, the moon is further away and therefore looks smaller. As a result, the circumference of the sun will appear as a much larger and brighter ring of light, called an *annulus*, around the silhouette of the moon. A 'hybrid eclipse,' the rarest form, fluctuates between the appearance of a total and an annular eclipse while the final category is the 'partial eclipse,' which is much more commonly seen and occurs when the moon hides only a part of the sun. This happens when the moon is not exactly in conjunction with the sun or if a total solar eclipse is being viewed outside of the moon's umbra.

Although a total solar eclipse occurs on average every 18 months in various positions across the Earth, it is estimated that 370 years must pass before any one particular position on our planet will be able to witness another of these spectacular events. For those who see one, a total eclipse is a breathtaking reminder of the vast scale of our solar system.

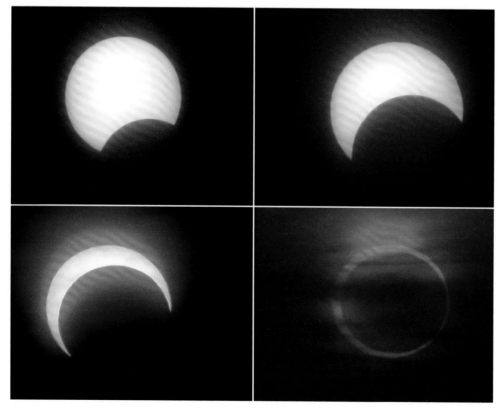

Opposite page: *A total solar eclipse, showing solar flares and prominences past the limb of the Sun, which is blocked by the Moon, and the solar corona. This eclipse took place during a maximum of a sunspot cycle, and the image is processed to show not only the corona but also the chromosphere and the prominences.*

Left: *A combination picture taken on January 15, 2010 showing different phases of an annular solar eclipse in Lianyungang, China.*

STATUE OF LIBERTY

Bartholdi's design was for a truly colossal work. Liberty herself is 46 meters (151 ft) tall, and made from copper over a steel frame, while the torch's flame is covered with gold leaf. Liberty's head is topped with a crown from which radiate seven spikes, said to symbolize the seven continents of the world. The crown recalls the Colossus of Rhodes, which was thought to have had a similar crown. That ancient wonder of the world is also remembered in the poem by Emma Lazarus, entitled 'The New Colossus' which adorns the pedestal and contains one of the world's most famous lines of poetry: 'Give me your tired, your poor, your huddled masses yearning to breathe free…'

Due to delays in financing the project, on both sides of the Atlantic, Liberty did not arrive in New York in time for the centennial, but by July 1884 work on the statue was completed in France. Two years later, on April 22, 1886, with the statue already arrived in the city, the pedestal was finished. Over the following months Liberty was reassembled at her new home and on October 28, 1886, she was unveiled by President Grover Cleveland amid fireworks and celebrations.

Today, Liberty is one of New York City's, and America's, favorite icons. Her image adorns all manner of souvenirs, postcards and T-shirts, and the statue itself is visited by millions of tourists each year, many of whom buy tickets to climb up inside and take in the views from Liberty's crown.

Now recognized around the globe as a symbol of hope, New York City's Statue of Liberty once offered the first glimpse of America to many immigrants. Holding aloft the torch of enlightenment, carrying a tablet on which is written the date of the Declaration of Independence, and trampling broken chains beneath her left foot, Liberty welcomed them with the promise of freedom.

Standing 93 meters (305 ft) above New York Harbor, on Liberty Island, the Statue of Liberty – or 'Liberty Enlightening the World' to give the statue its proper title – was a gift to the American nation from the people of France. Intended to mark the centennial of the signing of the Declaration of Independence, which fell in 1876, it was designed by French Sculptor Frédéric Bartholdi and funded by public donations, charitable events and a lottery. Similar events in the United States raised the money required to build Liberty's pedestal. Bartholdi himself helped pick the site for his work, an island formerly known as Bedloe's Island, close to Ellis Island, which would – from 1892 onward – become the gateway into the United States for millions of immigrants.

Main image: *Holding her torch aloft, above New York Harbor, the Statue of Liberty is an international symbol of American democracy and freedom.*

Inset: *A popular myth has it that the sculptor Frédéric Bartholdi modeled Liberty's noble face on his own mother's though he never, in fact, confirmed this.*

STONEHENGE

Great Britain has almost 1,000 stone circles, but Stonehenge is undoubtedly the greatest of them. Located 3.2 kilometers (2 miles) from the town of Amesbury in the county of Wiltshire, it comprises a system of earthworks around the famous standing stones. Scattered around the area are hundreds of burial mounds dating back to Neolithic times.

The henge was built in stages, the first of which was a simple circular ditch with raised banks, constructed about 3100 BC. A ring of pits suggests that a wooden circle may have been positioned about the same time and archeologists believe that the site was used as a cemetery. Around 2600 BC, the circle builders began using stone instead of timber, probably bringing 80 3.6-tonne (4-ton) 'bluestones' from a site in Wales (though it has recently been suggested that the stones might have been 'dropped' closer to Stonehenge by ice age glaciers). At the center, Stonehenge's builders placed a 5.4-tonne (6-ton), sandstone altar stone.

Around 200 years later, 30 great sarsen stones were bought to the site and arranged in a circle with a diameter of 33 meters (108 ft) and fitted with lintels that were fixed to

Shrouded in the mystery of 5,000 years, Stonehenge is one of the world's most recognized landmarks and a marvel of ancient engineering. Built of huge blocks, many of which were dragged over 250 kilometers (160 miles) to the site, it is precisely arranged and is a testament to its builders' sophisticated knowledge of geometry and astronomy. There are no records of who built it, or why, and it has become associated with many wild myths and legends, as well as scientific and archeological theories.

one another with tongue and groove joints. Weighing about 22 tonnes (25 tons) each, the new circle (with the lintels in place) stood 4.9 meters (16 ft) above the ground and the standing stones were subtly worked to mitigate the effects of perspective. Five more 'trilathons' – two standing stones supporting a lintel – were erected in a horseshoe shape within the circle. Each stone used in the trilathons weighs roughly 45 tonnes (50 tons) and the tallest trilathon would have measured about 7.3 meters (24 ft).

Myth and folklore hold various characters including Merlin and the Devil responsible for building Stonehenge and using it for magical purposes. It is also a popular belief that the circle was used by druids, though this is unlikely: druids are known to have conducted their rituals in sacred groves rather than around such circles. In fact, it is more likely that Stonehenge served as a calendar and observatory. It is perfectly aligned to the sunrise in midsummer and sunset in midwinter and can be used to chart the rising and setting of the moon, an incredible achievement for a Neolithic culture. This does not necessarily mean that Stonehenge did not also have a ritual or religious significance, however. In ancient times scientific and religious pursuits were not separated as they are now.

Today, the site remains a unique and magnificent part of the British landscape and one that still inspires awe. It is owned by the British Crown and strictly managed, though modern-day druids are regularly allowed to conduct their rituals here.

Main image: *Only three of the large central trilathons remain complete, though the single standing stone to the center right gives an indication of how tall the largest of the group would have been.*

Inset: *An aerial view of Stonehenge showing the outside ring of sarsen stones with the remains of the five great trilathons within.*

Following pages: *The standing stones of Stonehenge, silhouetted against a glorious sunset.*

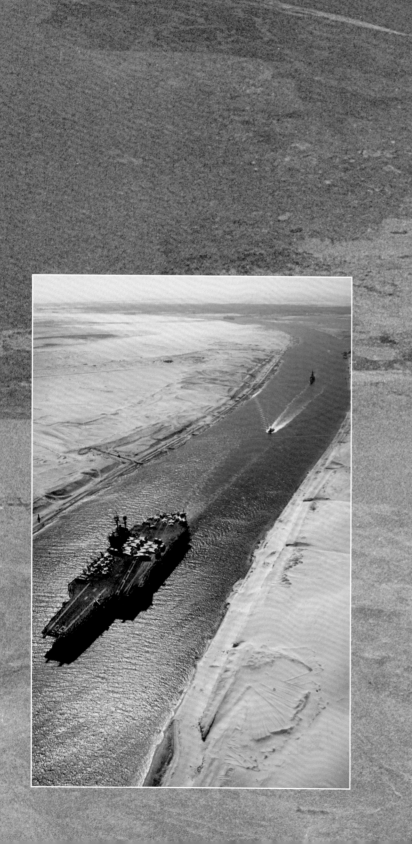

SUEZ CANAL

Situated on the Isthmus of Suez, at the point where Africa meets Asia, the Suez Canal is a marvel of engineering that stretches just over 193 kilometers (120 miles) between the Mediterranean Sea to the Gulf of Suez and the Red Sea.

The history of canal building in the area stretches back over almost 4,000 years. The trade possibilities of a waterway connecting Europe to Asia were recognized by Ancient Egyptians and the first ruler to attempt to build a canal in the region was the pharaoh Senusret II, who ruled between 1897 and 1878 BC. Although, in all likelihood, he failed to complete a channel, remains of excavations that may have been part of this great ancient undertaking were found in the mid-19th century. A later canal, built under Necho II (610–595 BC) connected the Great Bitter Lake, a saltwater lake through which the modern canal passes, to a branch of the River Nile and, hence, the Mediterranean. The building effort is said to have cost 100,000 lives, but still did not complete the link to the Red Sea. The first to do so was Ptolemy II (285–246 BC), creating a complete waterway between East and West. Intermittently falling into disuse, it was dredged and restored by various regional powers for about 1,000 years before the last boat navigated its length.

Although Napoleon Bonaparte revived interest in building a new canal at the end of the 18th century, sending out engineers and cartographers to the region in 1798, it was not until the mid-19th century that technical details were ironed out and permission obtained from the Egyptian Viceroy Sa'id Pasha. Built by the Suez Canal Company – an Egyptian Corporation formed by the French developer Ferdinand de Lesseps and primarily owned by French shareholders – the modern canal opened on November 17, 1869. The result of ten years of work using the labor of about 1.5 million people in total, it was originally a 164 kilometers (102 miles) long, single-lane channel that incorporated places where ships could safely pass in the Great Bitter Lake and at Ballah By-Pass. Since enlarged, to the north – on the Mediterranean – is Port Said while Port Tawfiq, near the city of Suez, marks the canal's southern terminus. It is a sea-level canal with no locks, a current depth of 20 meters (66 ft), and a width of between 205 to 225 meters (670–740 ft), sufficient to allow passage to all but the very largest of supertankers.

Today, about 20,000 ships use the Suez Canal each year, paying an average toll of US$250,000. Allowing vessels access to the Indian Ocean and the Far East and cutting thousands of kilometers from the journey around the treacherous waters off Africa's southern tip, the Suez Canal is one of the world's most heavily used sea lanes.

Main image: *The Suez Canal connects the Mediterranean to the Gulf of Suez. About two thirds of the way along the canal, to the south, the Great Bitter Lake provides a passing place for ships.*

Inset: *The 81,000-tonne (90,000-ton) aircraft carrier, USS Nimitz, maneuvers through the Suez Canal.*

SYDNEY OPERA HOUSE

In 2003, Jørn Utzon – the architect who designed the Sydney Opera House – was awarded the Pritzker Prize, architecture's highest accolade. Presented to a living architect whose vision and work has helped reshape the world's perception of architectural possibilities, the citation certificate described Australia's most iconic building as his masterpiece and 'an image of great beauty that has become known throughout the world – a symbol for not only a city, but a whole country and continent.' Such high praise for the Opera House has been echoed by many. One of the world's foremost architectural grandees, Eero Saarinen, called the design 'genius' when he saw it for the first time and, 50 years later, in 2007, UNESCO designated it a World Heritage Site, making Utzon only the second person to receive such an honor within their own lifetime.

Discussions about building an opera house in Australia's largest city began in the late 1940s, with Joseph Cahill, the Premier of New South Wales, announcing a competition for designs in 1955. From the 233 entries, the Danish architect Jørn Utzon's was selected in 1957, having been – it is reported – picked out of the already rejected entries by Saarinen.

By 1959, the construction site on Sydney's Bennelong Point was prepared and building began with the podium, despite the fact that Utzon had not yet finalized the design. The series of 'shells' that give the Opera House its distinctive appearance

came next but proved problematic. Because nothing similar had ever been attempted before – and the architect had not been allowed to finish his plans before work commenced – Utzon's original plan for constructing them was found to be too expensive. Between 1957 and 1963, no less than 12 redesigns took place before a final form and construction solution was found and implemented. As work on the shells neared completion in 1965, a series of political rows broke out with the new Minister of Public Works, Davis Hughes, who had been appointed that year. Hughes had long been opposed to the building, and forced Utzon's resignation from the project in 1966. The architect never returned, and construction was completed in 1973 under Peter Hall, aided by several other architects and designers.

Sydney Opera House was opened by Queen Elizabeth II on October 20, 1973. With its audacious curving peaks resembling billowing sails, it is without doubt one of the world's most distinctive buildings. Housing six separate performance spaces of various sizes, from the grand Concert Hall which seats 2,678 to the outdoor Forecourt venue, it is a magnificent confection of modern design that hosts more than 1,500 performances every year, which are attended by about 1.2 million people.

Main image: *Sydney Opera House stands on Bennelong Point, which was originally a small island and later became the site of Fort Macquarie. The old fort was razed to make way for the Opera House.*

Inset: *Often likened to the sails of a ship, the shells of the Opera House roof are made of 4,000 panels fixed to 2,400 precast ribs.*

TABLE MOUNTAIN

Standing magnificent above the South African city of Cape Town is one of the world's most instantly recognizable mountains. Like Kilimanjaro, Table Mountain has become an African icon, and is an unusual peak that rises in steep craggy cliffs to an almost flat plateau. Often swathed in clouds that have been likened to a tablecloth, the mountain creates a spectacular backdrop for the city at its base and is an ecological wonderland that harbors a variety of unique plant life.

Located at the southern tip of the African continent, overlooking South Africa's second most populous city and the wide Table Bay, Table Mountain is the area's most prominent landmark. It reaches 1,086 meters (3,563 ft) at its highest point, where a stone cairn called Maclear's Beacon stands near its eastern end – this is just 19 meters (62 ft) higher than the western end of the plateau 3 kilometers (2 miles) away. The mountain is also flanked by two distinctive peaks: the sharp summit of Devil's Peak to the east and Lion's Head to the west. The steep cliffs of the mountain are divided by Platteklip Gorge, meaning 'flat stone gorge.' This chasm provides the most direct and least arduous climb to the summit and was the path taken by Antonio de Saldanha (who gave the mountain its name) for the first recorded climb in 1503. On top of the plateau are the remains of three defensive forts, called 'blockhouses,' built by the British at the end of the 18th century as well as a terminal for the Table Mountain Cableway, which was first built in the 1920s.

The landscape of the mountain is enriched by many indigenous plants and animals. In fact, Table Mountain supports over 2,200 species of plants, many of which are unique to the area. The animals which make their home on Table Mountain are not as numerous as they once were, and larger species such as lions and leopards have disappeared completely, but there are still some fine examples of local fauna. Most commonly seen is the rock hyrax. Resembling a large guinea pig, these creatures have adapted well to the influx of tourists and stick to areas where they might find food (or be given some). Other species include porcupines, mongooses, snakes and tortoises.

Since the 1990s, the mountain and its surrounding area have become a national park, and today it is one of South Africa's most popular tourist attractions, welcoming hundreds of thousands of hikers, rock climbers and sightseers every year. Table Mountain is also unique in having a constellation named for it, *Mensa* ('table'), which appears beneath Orion in the skies of the Southern Hemisphere.

Main image: *A view of Table Mountain with the city of Cape Town at its feet. Winds rising up the mountain slopes often condense into a 'table cloth' of cloud.*

Inset: *The flanks of Table Mountain provide an ecosystem that is home to a diverse variety of animal life and many hundreds of plant species.*

TAIPEI 101

At 509.2 meters (1,670.2 ft) from ground level to the tip of its spire, Taipei 101 was the tallest building in the world between its completion in 2004 until Burj Khalifa in Dubai was officially opened in early 2010. A remarkable structure inspired by the traditional Chinese pagoda, and incorporating many other Chinese symbols within its design, the skyscraper has won numerous awards, including the Emporis Skyscraper Award 2004 and the *Popular Science* magazine 2004 Best of What's New Engineering Award. In 2005, the Discovery Channel named it as one of the Seven Wonders of Engineering and the following year *Newsweek* magazine proclaimed the tower one of the Seven New Wonders of the World.

Located in Taipei City, on the island of Taiwan, and designed by C. Y. Lee and Partners, Taipei 101 was the first skyscraper ever to top the height of half a kilometer. As well as breaking the record with the height to the top of its spire, it held the tallest building records for ground to the top of its roof at 449.2 meters (1,474 ft), and to the highest occupied floor, which is 439.2 meters (1,441 ft) above ground.

Constructed in an area that is prone to earthquakes and fierce monsoons, its design incorporated innovative strengthening techniques, which combine to make it among the safest skyscrapers ever built. Below ground its foundations are supported by 380 piles that reach 80 meters (262 ft) into the earth while, above ground, the tower's 101 floors rest on 36 steel columns, eight of which are classed as 'mega-columns'

Main image: *Taipei 101 dominates the dusk skyline of the Xinyi District in Taipei.*

Inset: *The tower's 101 floors represent both the binary system of modern technology and great ambition in aiming higher than 100, a number that the Chinese associate with perfection.*

and are further strengthened with concrete. Taipei 101 also contains a huge 'tuned mass dampener,' a giant spherical pendulum that hangs from the 92nd to 88th floor and which sways to offset movement in the building caused by strong winds.

For its builders, the symbolic concept of Taipei 101 was just as important as the technology involved in its construction. In fact, the building abounds with symbolism and is a superb expression of Chinese culture past and present. From about a third of the way up it rises in eight stepped sections – eight is a lucky number by the Chinese – each of which slants outward slightly. This recalls both the style of Chinese pagodas, and also the bamboo plant, which is a symbol of strength, growth and learning. Elsewhere, the Chinese *ruyi* symbol of fulfillment and protection is used as a design feature.

Unique and unmistakably Chinese, Taipei 101 remains one of the world's most exceptional skyscrapers. With an outdoor observatory deck on the 91st floor, it also offers outstanding views across the city and is a popular destination for tourists.

TAJ MAHAL

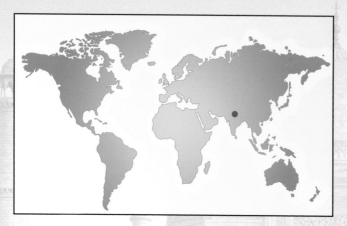

The Indian continent in the mid-17th century was dominated by the Islamic Mughal Empire, and was beginning to experience a cultural and artistic 'golden age,' that blended traditional Indian designs with Islamic forms – and those of Persia, from where the Mughal rulers' ancestors came. The most perfect example of this new style is also one of the world's most famous buildings: the Taj Mahal. Built by the Emperor Shah Jahan as a huge, ornate memorial to his favorite wife, it is an unmatched architectural pearl. A breathtakingly beautiful structure of white marble with exquisite detailing and crowned with a perfectly proportioned dome, the mausoleum is widely regarded as one of the world's finest buildings.

Located in Agra in the north of India, the Taj Mahal was completed around 1653. Its story stretches back to 1631 though,

when Mumtaz Mahal died while giving birth to Shah Jahan's 14th child. The emperor and his wife had been inseparable since they had fallen in love at first sight as teenagers. On his wife's death, the emperor's grief was so great that he became determined to build the most exquisite monument to her that the world had ever seen.

Construction began almost immediately and, over 22 years, 1,000 elephants and 22,000 laborers and craftsmen worked on the building. The mausoleum itself was finished in 1648 with the outbuildings and gardens completed five years later.

The finished building is stunning. It stands atop a plinth, bounded by four minarets, and rises to the famous onion dome, which is tipped with a lotus design. Exterior walls are carved with abstract forms and flowers, or decorated with passages from the Koran in black marble. Before the building was plundered by British troops in the mid-19th century, the walls were also set with precious and semi-precious stones. The gardens feature a reflecting pool and were originally laid out with fountains, avenues and abundant plants and flowers, though they were changed to suit British tastes in the 19th century.

Inside, the Taj Mahal is even more richly ornamented. The somber, plain crypt, where Shah Jahan and Mumtaz Jahan lie side by side, facing Mecca, is beneath a main chamber that contains false tombs – a feature that was common in Mughal burial places as Islam requires the actual tomb to be free of decoration. Arches, columns, balconies, screens and walls are richly carved with bas-reliefs or inlaid with designs in lapis lazuli and other precious stones, while perforated marble screens give the light a shadowy, 'dappled' effect. The exterior themes are carried through into the interior with calligraphy praising Mumtaz Jahan and repeating Koranic verses.

A UNESCO World Heritage Site since 1983, the Taj Mahal was voted one of the New Seven Wonders of the World in 2007. It is also one of the world's most popular tourist sights, attracting between three and four million people annually.

Opposite page: *The white marbled domes of the Taj Mahal shimmer in the waters of the reflecting pool. The pool is called* al Hawd al-Kawathar *and represents the 'Tank of Abundance' promised to Mohammad.*

Left: *The intricately carved façade of the Taj Mahal is decorated with a mixture of calligraphy, abstract forms or plant motifs but no depictions of people as these are forbidden under Islamic tradition.*

TEOTIHUACAN

Although it is now impossible to be sure who built it, over 1,000 years ago Teotihuacan was one of the greatest cities on Earth and exerted an influence over the development of many other Mesoamerican cultures, including the Mayans and Aztecs. Now, the grand pyramids and the temples that line the Avenue of the Dead are frequented by archeologists and tourists, though the mysterious city still stands as a testament to the glories, and cruelty, of an extinct culture.

Located 48 kilometers (30 miles) northeast of Mexico City, Teotihuacan is one of the world's greatest archeological sites and a superb example of pre-Columbian architecture. Although archeologists disagree about who built the city — even its original name is unknown — it is generally believed that the area was settled about 200 BC. Sprawling over a site of 22 square kilometers (8.5 sq miles), at its peak during the first half of the new millennium the city was home to roughly 200,000 people of various cultures.

Around the time of Christ, the population had increased to around 80,000 and a period of monumental building works began. Centered on the Avenue of the Dead, numerous temples were raised as well as two great pyramids. The Pyramid of the Sun was begun around the year 100 AD. It is 75 meters

(246 ft) high with a base width of 225 meters (733 ft). The huge structure was topped with an altar and covered with plaster, which would have been decorated with bright paintings, though these have long since disappeared. Beneath the pyramid is a natural tunnel that leads to a cave that is said to have been a royal tomb and at each corner archeologists have unearthed the grave of a child, believed to have been sacrificed during the building work.

At the end of the Avenue of the Dead, the Pyramid of the Moon stands over the Plaza of the Moon, which is lined with smaller temples and platforms. Smaller than the Pyramid of the Sun, at 42 meters (138 ft) high and a base width of 150 meters (492 ft), the pyramid was built from about 200 AD onward, in as many as seven stages over about 200 years. Each stage was celebrated with a ritual bloodletting. Within the pyramid, archeologists have so far located five tombs, each filled with sacrificial victims, both human and animal.

At the opposite end of the Avenue of the Dead is an area known as the Citadel, which would have once been the political center of the city as well as the heart of its religious activities. This part of the city is home to Teotihuacan's third-largest pyramid, known as the Temple of the Feathered Serpent, beneath which the bodies of over 200 human sacrifices have been found.

Monumental and endlessly fascinating, no one is sure why Teotihuacan society collapsed in the 7th or 8th century, though archeologists have found evidence of an uprising possibly caused by famine. Today, the city is a UNESCO World Heritage Site and one of Mexico's most visited places.

Main image: *Looking out across Teotihuacan from the Pyramid of the Moon down the Avenue of the Dead. To the left is the Pyramid of the Sun.*

Inset: *The Temple of the Feathered Serpent is decorated with many representations of the ancient Mayan god, Quetzalcoatl.*

Following pages: *The great Pyramid of the Sun is the largest of the pyramid structures in Teotihuacan and bears the name given to it long after the city was abandoned. Like the city itself, its original name is now lost.*

TERRACOTTA ARMY

In 1974, farmers on the outskirts of Xi'an, in China's Shaanxi Province were drilling a well when they made a surprising discovery. Instead of hitting water, they unearthed ancient bronze weapons and parts of figures made of terracotta. Further excavation over the following two years revealed an astonishing underground system of trenches, which contained what soon came to be called the 'Eighth Wonder of the Ancient World.' With an overall area of 22,000 square meters (237,000 square ft), the pits held 8,000 life-size terracotta warriors lined up in battle formation, 130 chariots, 150 cavalry and a further 520 horses.

The Terracotta Army was made in 210 BC to accompany Qin Shi Huang, the first emperor of a unified China, into the afterlife in order that he would have the troops to conquer an empire in Heaven as he had on Earth. Situated close by his, as yet unexcavated, mausoleum (which is thought to be the largest ever built), the pits where the terracotta troops were interred are between 5 to 7 meters (16 and 23 ft) below the present surface level and are arranged in trenches divided by earth walls and floored with bricks. Rafters between the dividing walls supported mats onto which was piled earth, concealing the army below the ground for almost 2,200 years before the group of farmers accidentally drilled into one.

The figures themselves are extremely lifelike and were assembled from constituent parts that were made from molds before having individual features added. The artisans were careful to create expressions on each of the soldiers, giving each a unique personality. When finished they were painted and lacquered, though only a few of the pieces still have any traces of their original colors. They do, however, bear the marks of the workshops that produced them. On completion, the figures were placed in the pit according to rank, ready to engage the enemy. Originally armed with real weapons, including crossbows, spears and halberds, the troops are made up of standing and kneeling archers, armored and unarmored foot soldiers as well as cavalrymen standing by their horses and charioteers – though the chariots were made of wood and have disintegrated. The smallest of the three pits was found to contain only 68 figures when it was unearthed in 1976 and the arrangement of the armies in the two main pits suggest that this was intended as a command post.

Today, the site is one of China's most important historical locations and a UNESCO World Heritage Site. Its incredible pottery warriors are protected beneath specially made covers and attract hundreds of thousands of visitors each year. Nevertheless, many archeologists believe that the Terracotta Army offers only a glimpse of what may be hidden beneath the ground in the area. It is thought that thousands more warriors may still remain undiscovered and that the mausoleum of the emperor himself might contain even greater treasures.

Main image: *Known as 'Qin's Armies' the terracotta warriors were built to defend their master's nearby necropolis and to follow their emperor into the afterlife.*

Inset: *Although foot soldiers are by far the most numerous of the emperor's army, it also includes superbly detailed generals, strongmen, musicians and many extremely lifelike horses.*

THINGVELLIR NATIONAL PARK

Starkly lovely, and a site of immense historical and archeological importance, Thingvellir National Park represents the cradle of Iceland's national culture. Home of the country's government and law court from 930 AD until 1789, fragments of the past still dot a landscape that is as rich in natural beauty as it is in Norse history.

The name 'Thingvellir' means 'parliament plains' in Icelandic, and in its native country is spelled with the 'Th' replaced by the Icelandic symbol, þ. It received the name during a period of Viking settlement that began in about 800 AD and ended toward the middle of the 11th century. By the beginning of the 10th century, Iceland's swelling population recognized the need for a general assembly that would replace the small regional assemblies that had sprung up and serve the governmental and legal needs of the entire island. Known as an *Althing* (again the 'th' is spelled with the same special character in Icelandic), it was decided that the assembly should meet each year on lands that had recently been confiscated to punish their former owner, who had murdered his servant. Abundant in good pasture, water and firewood while being relatively easy to reach from anywhere on the island, the undulating hills and flat plains of the region, bounded by rocky cliffs, were considered ideal.

The assembly's focal point was the Lögberg ('Law Rock'), a natural stone platform. From here, the Law Speaker – who was elected for a three-year tenure – would recite the laws of the land from memory, and also preside over legislative decisions and law cases as well as ruling on other matters of importance to the young nation. It was from here, for instance, that in the year 1000 the Law Speaker publicly announced the country's adoption of Christianity, among chaotic scenes.

In 1262, Iceland fell under Norwegian rule and the *Althing* became simply a court of law. Its power dwindled further under Danish rule from 1662 onward, and the final assembly took place in 1798. Over nine centuries it had become a place of vital importance to Icelanders. Not simply a center of law and government, but a marketplace and cultural hub. Today, the remains of those times can be seen in the ruined rock and turf huts used by visitors.

Thingvellir became Iceland's first national park in 1930 and was placed on the UNESCO World Heritage list in 2004 due to the unique role it played in the development of Norse culture. Today, it remains a national treasure and its great beauty and rich heritage also helps to make it one of Iceland's most popular tourist destinations.

Main image: *Now Iceland's most treasured national park, Thingvellir was for centuries the cultural and political hub of the nation.*

Inset: *The location of the Law Rock is still argued over, though a flagpole now marks the flat ledge that is thought to be the most likely spot.*

TIKAL

Surrounded by the lush tropical rainforests of the Petén Basin in northern Guatemala, the ancient Mayan city of Tikal dates back to 400 BC and was once the hub of the most powerful Mayan kingdom in Mesoamerican history. The largest of the remaining Mayan cities – dominated by steep-sided stepped temples, pyramids, and palaces – for centuries Tikal was concealed by jungle. For this reason it remains extremely well preserved, offering rare insights into a fascinating civilization.

Although evidence suggests that farmers had been working the land in the area where Tikal stands since 1000 BC, major construction work, such as the creation of Tikal's pyramids and platforms, began around 400 BC. Over the following centuries, Tikal's influence increased and the burgeoning city rose in status, aided by the collapse of other Mayan towns such as neighboring El Mirador and by the establishment of a powerful royal dynasty in the 3rd century AD. Despite the fact that it was often at war with other Mayan city-states, Tikal flourished into a large, vibrant metropolis. Toward the end of the 4th century, however, it was conquered by the great city of Teotihuacan. Despite suffering defeat and the execution of its native king, the city was soon thriving again, fostering close trading ties and becoming a supportive ally to the invaders. By the middle of the 5th century, Tikal dominated the area around the Petén Basin and covered an area of 25 square kilometers (9 sq miles), boasting fortifications that encompassed a territory of about 120 square kilometers (46 sq miles).

What remains of this great metropolis is an impressive collection of limestone ruins, including temples, palaces, pyramids, residences, statues, platforms and even a jailhouse. The most famous structures are the six enormous step pyramids, some of which reach heights of over 60 meters (200 ft) and are topped with temples. Temple I, also known as the Temple of the Great Jaguar, is the tomb of Jasaw Chan K'awil, the 26th ruler of Tikal. The edifice was completed between 740 and 750 AD and contained offerings of food and drink, jade ornaments and ornately carved human and animal bones.

Tikal remained a regional power until the 10th century, when evidence suggests that the Mayan civilization underwent a collapse – possibly due to famine – and population fell into sharp decline. Having been at the center of Mayan culture and politics for a millennium, the city was abandoned to the jungle, its grand plaza left to a few squatters and its awe-inspiring temples looted.

European explorers were first guided to the 'lost city' by natives in the mid-19th century. By the beginning of the 20th century the site had become renowned as an archeological wonder. Now a UNESCO World Heritage Site, surrounded by its own National Park and with an on-site museum, Tikal's astonishing architecture and grand history attract many tourists as well as archeologists.

Opposite page: *The Temple of the Great Jaguar in Tikal, like other pyramids on the site, is impressive, though archeologists have estimated that each took less than two years to complete.*

Left: *The North Acropolis of Tikal has buildings dating back to 350 BC. Over the following centuries royal temples, pyramids and stone columns were added, many carved with hieroglyphic texts.*

TONGARIRO NATIONAL PARK

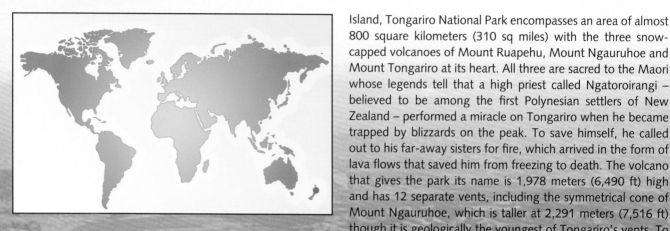

The first national park to be established in New Zealand, Tongariro is not only a landscape of great beauty, dominated by the peaks of active volcanoes, but is also of great cultural importance to the Maori people. For this reason, it was the first ever place to be inscribed on the UNESCO World Heritage list as a dual ecological and cultural site.

Located at the center of New Zealand's North Island, Tongariro National Park encompasses an area of almost 800 square kilometers (310 sq miles) with the three snow-capped volcanoes of Mount Ruapehu, Mount Ngauruhoe and Mount Tongariro at its heart. All three are sacred to the Maori whose legends tell that a high priest called Ngatoroirangi – believed to be among the first Polynesian settlers of New Zealand – performed a miracle on Tongariro when he became trapped by blizzards on the peak. To save himself, he called out to his far-away sisters for fire, which arrived in the form of lava flows that saved him from freezing to death. The volcano that gives the park its name is 1,978 meters (6,490 ft) high and has 12 separate vents, including the symmetrical cone of Mount Ngauruhoe, which is taller at 2,291 meters (7,516 ft) though it is geologically the youngest of Tongariro's vents. To the south is Ruapehu, which rises to 2,797 meters (9,177 ft) and is the highest on North Island. All the park's volcanoes

are highly active and early warning systems have been put in place to evacuate skiers and hikers in the event of an impending eruption.

The lower slopes of the volcanoes are heavily forested while elsewhere in the park are great spreading tree ferns, old lava flows and tussock grassland. There are also hanging highland lakes made a vivid emerald green by mineral deposits, alien landscapes of rock turned deep red by oxidized copper and gushing streams and waterfalls. The park is home to many species of rare birds as well as animals including the only mammals native to New Zealand – short and long-tailed bats – as well as many species introduced by European colonists, such as deer and rabbits. Some of these imported species have proved devastating to the park's finely balanced ecology.

The flightless kiwi bird, for example, was nearly wiped out when stoats arrived and began to feed on their eggs, while heather, which was planted to provide grouse moors for shooting parties, has spread widely and proven difficult to eradicate.

Today, the park is one of New Zealand's most popular attractions. Its spectacular beauty attracts thousands of hikers each year, who have more recently been joined by many people eager to visit the fantastic scenes of Peter Jackson's *Lord of the Rings* trilogy. The park is also used for various outdoor sports, including kayaking and mountain biking as well as skiing.

Main image: *The misty summit of Mount Ruapehu, one of the world's most active volcanoes, in Tongariro National Park.*

Inset: *Mount Ngauruhoe, the youngest of Tongariro's volcanoes, first erupted 2,500 years ago and exploded 45 times during the 20th century. Ngauruhoe achieved worldwide fame as Mount Doom in Peter Jackson's film version of The Lord of the Rings.*

ULURU (AYERS ROCK)

Sacred to Australia's Aboriginal people and one of the world's most recognized landmarks, the vast bulk of Uluru is a spectacular, unexpected feature amid the flat Northern Territory desert. Formed of sandstone that seems to glow a deep red during sunset, and dotted with life-giving springs of water, it is easy to understand why the ancient people who lived here formed a mystical attachment to the rock. Today, it is still possible to see evidence of the Anangu people's 'dreamtime' beliefs in Uluru's cliffs and caves, which are marked with the paintings of their distant ancestors.

Located in the deep southwest of Australia's Northern Territory, almost in the center of the continent, Uluru is an isolated island of rock, known as an 'inselberg.' Formed over hundreds of millions of years, it represents one of the few remnants of what was once a great range of sandstone plates that were tipped almost vertical by geological forces, then

eroded by wind and water. In fact, like an iceberg, the greater part of the rock still lies beneath the ground. It is 9.4 kilometers (5.8 miles) in circumference around the base and rises to a height of 348 meters (1,141 ft), with an area of 3.33 square kilometers (1.29 sq miles), and now stands within Uluru-Kata Tjuta National Park.

Archeologists believe that humans have lived in the vicinity for over 10,000 years and for the Anangu people the rock became central to the dreamtime tradition; a sacred dreamtime track twists up its slopes. The Anangu see evidence of their creator spirits in the physical attributes of the rock, including a series of shallow bowls which were said to have been formed by Tatji, the small Red Lizard, throwing down his *kali* (a throwing stick). Within many caves dreamtime stories are painted on the walls and have been renewed many times over the millennia.

The first European to see the rock was the explorer William Gosse who arrived here in July 1873, and gave it the name Ayers Rock after Sir Henry Ayers, then the Chief Secretary of South Australia. Since then, the site has been the subject of numerous controversies between the Aboriginal people and colonists. Although it was part of the Aboriginal Reserve for a time, the area was taken back by the Australian government in 1958 when it was realized that Ayers Rock had become a popular tourist attraction. It was, however, placed back in Aboriginal hands in 1985, and became a UNESCO World Heritage Site in 1987. Today, the Anangu prefer visitors not to climb Uluru – though many ignore the request – but it continues to attract hundreds of thousands of tourists each year.

Main image: *As the setting sun hits the rock of Uluru, it appears to glow bright red. In fact, the shade of the sandstone seems to change over the entire day and, during rainy periods, seems to become silver as the water flows across it.*

Inset: *Uluru has many ancient rock paintings depicting important motifs of well known 'dreamtime' stories.*

VALLEY OF THE KINGS

For a period of 500 years, the pharaohs of Egypt, and the most powerful nobles, were buried in tombs cut into a valley in the Theban Hills on the west bank of the Nile. With them were interred stores of treasures and goods to sustain them in the afterlife. Although most were subsequently robbed, one remained pristine: the resting place of the minor boy-king, Tutankhamen. When it was opened in 1922, the world was astonished by the wealth found within. What riches were contained in the tombs of greater pharaohs can only be imagined.

The Valley of the Kings lies in southern Egypt (or Upper Egypt as the Ancient Egyptians called it) across the Nile from the city of Luxor. Between the 16th and 11th centuries BC, during the time of a great Egyptian cultural resurgence known as the New Kingdom, it served as a royal necropolis. Into its barren, pale limestone cliffs were dug 63 tombs (that have been so far discovered) ranging from single plain pits and chambers to subterranean complexes with over 100 rooms. Most consist of a long corridor that slopes downward, passing through a series of chambers before terminating with the room where the sarcophagus (stone coffin) would have been placed. They are decorated throughout with murals and carvings that depict sacred texts and funeral traditions. During the funeral rites, the tombs would have been filled with all the pharaoh might need or desire in the afterlife – including simple items of clothing as

well as treasure – then sealed and plugged with rubble and the entrance carefully camouflaged.

As the power of the pharaohs waned toward the end of the New Kingdom, the tombs of their ancestors became increasingly targeted by thieves. Although many were caught and harshly punished, the treasures of the pharaohs were never replaced and, at some point, the royal mummies were moved to (at least) two caches close by for their protection. The most famous of these is known as the cache of Deir el-Bahri. It was found to contain the rewrapped and carefully marked mummies of 40 Egyptian royals including that of Ramesses II (the famous Ramesses the Great) as well as lesser nobility, when it was rediscovered in 1881.

Nevertheless, a very few tombs in the Valley of the Kings escaped being completely emptied by robbers, including that of Tutankhamen. When the British archeologist Howard Carter entered the resting place of the boy-king in 1922, he found that, while the tomb had been pillaged at least twice in the past, 3,500 artifacts remained and the pharaoh's 'nested' sarcophagus was undisturbed. When opened it was revealed to contain the fabulous gold funeral mask that now resides in Cairo's Egyptian Museum.

The Valley of the Kings now welcomes thousands of visitors each day and has been a tourist attraction for many hundreds of years. In fact, many tombs bear the graffiti of ancient Greek and Roman travelers. While the pharaohs may have been robbed of their treasures, and moved away, within the dark, richly adorned corridors and chambers of their tombs, it is still possible to sense the great power and mystery of one of the world's great vanished civilizations.

Main image: *Unlike the grand pyramids and funeral temples of the Egyptian Old and Middle Kingdoms, the tombs of later pharaohs were carefully hidden so that from afar, the Valley of the Kings looks unremarkable.*

Inset: *The spectacular funeral mask of Tutankhamen, discovered in the Valley of the Kings by Howard Carter in 1922, is made of solid gold inlaid with lapis lazuli, carnelian and glass.*

VERSAILLES PALACE

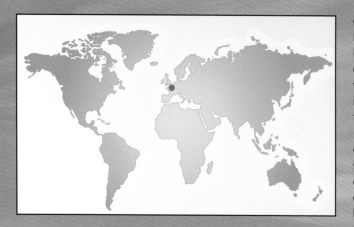

of Paris: a place where he could concentrate political power to himself and tighten his grip over the nation's affairs. In 1661, he settled on a hunting lodge near the village of Versailles and commissioned the architect Louis Le Vau to expand it. Le Vau's work, along with that of his successors, would eventually result in the finest architectural achievement of the age and one of the largest, most sumptuous palaces ever built.

Situated about 17 kilometers (10.5 miles) to the west of the center of Paris, the Palace of Versailles has a floor space of over 51,000 square meters (550,000 sq ft). Behind its vast, ornately carved façades, set with 2,153 windows, are 700 rooms. Many of these rooms – such as the famous Hall of Mirrors and the king's own apartments – are dazzlingly opulent and crammed with art treasures and magnificent furniture. The complex is set in exquisitely designed and manicured gardens of almost

In the mid-17th century the French King Louis XIV began looking for a place to establish a new court. He wanted somewhere close to, but set apart from, the crowds and turmoil

800 hectares (2,000 acres), containing 50 fountains, statues, a grand canal for boating parties and a magnificent grotto.

Le Vau oversaw two great construction projects that lasted between 1664 and 1672, by the end of which the grand apartments of the king and queen, which are perfectly matched, were completed. A third stage was conducted under the auspices of the great French architect Jules Hardouin-Mansart, during which the palace acquired much of its finished appearance with the addition of north and south wings and the Galerie des Glaces (Hall of Mirrors). The latter is quite breathtaking in its opulence and features 17 great arches, set with 21 mirrors each, that reflect great arched windows over-looking the gardens. Marble columns, vast chandeliers and rows of gilded sculpture ornament the hall. Unfortunately, other aspects of its original furnishings, which included tables of silver, were later removed to help pay for French military exploits. Elsewhere are other equally grand, though less renowned, salons and buildings such as L'Opéra, a private opera house and theater as well as

five chapels, of which the last to be built (it was consecrated in 1710) is widely held to be an architectural masterwork.

The royal family moved in during May 1682, and from that time Versailles became the absolute center of political power – and of intrigue and scandal – in France until the Revolution of 1789. Today, the Palace of Versailles and its grounds are a UNESCO World Heritage Site and one of France's greatest national treasures. Visited by millions of tourists each year, it is loved for it beauty but seen as a symbol of the extravagance of the French monarchy.

Main image: *Though building work was largely completed under Hardouin-Mansart, successive kings continued to make additions and remodel parts of Versailles.*

Inset: *The superb Hall of Mirrors is the most famous of Versailles' 700 rooms. Over 73 meters (239 ft) long, it was here that the Treaty of Versailles was signed, ending World War I.*

VICTORIA FALLS

Although neither the highest or the widest system of waterfalls in the world, the Victoria Falls have the longest, unbroken curtain of water anywhere on Earth. Tumbling 108 meters (354 ft) into a great chasm, the falls – 1,708 meters (5,604 ft) across – produce a constant roar and a cloud of vapor that rises 400 meters (1,312 ft) into the air. This vapor cloud led the indigenous people to name it *Mosi-oa-Tunya*, which translates as 'smoke that thunders.'

Abruptly interrupting the flow of Africa's Zambezi River between Zambia and Zimbabwe, Victoria Falls is a great crack in the Earth caused by a fracture in the basalt rock that lies beneath the region and further eroded by the water that pours over its edge. Known as the First Gorge, it is between 80 meters (262 ft) and 108 meters (354 ft) deep and, in places, just over 1,700 meters (5,600 ft) across. Into this chasm pour the waters of the Zambezi, resulting in an incredible waterfall three times as high as Niagara and over twice as wide as the Horseshoe Falls. Not only are the falls themselves an awe-inspiring spectacle, the spray that rises from the gorge can be seen from a distance of up to 50 kilometers (31 miles) away and, from a distance, resembles smoke pouring from the crater of an active volcano. During a full moon it also produces one of nature's most unexpected spectacles: night time rainbows, or 'moonbows' as they are known.

At the bottom of the gorge the turbulent waters of the Zambezi enter a system of tight zigzagging gorges that have been formed as the river recedes and mark the places where the falls once were. In fact, it is already possible to see where the next falls will form. At the section of the present falls known as the Devil's Cataract, a dip marks a weak fissure which, over thousands of years, will eventually be worn away to form a new waterfall.

The first European to see the falls was the explorer David Livingstone who reached them by canoe in 1855 and named them for the British queen. A century and a half later the falls attract hundreds of thousands of visitors each year, many of whom enjoy what must be the most exhilarating swim on the planet. At certain times of the year it is possible to reach a spot known as Devil's Pool from Livingstone Island on the waterfall's lip. Here, at the very edge of the falls, is a natural wall of stone just beneath the surface of the water that prevents swimmers from being carried over the edge.

Opposite page: *At times when the river is at less than full flood, small islets appear on the lip of the waterfall, dividing the great cascade into many parallel streams.*

Left: *The spray rising from the gorge creates constant rainbows throughout the day, and under certain conditions during the night as well.*

YELLOWSTONE NATIONAL PARK

On March 1, 1872, President Ulysses S. Grant signed a bill into law designating Yellowstone as the United States' first national park. Since then a further 57 have been created, but Yellowstone remains unique. While others may rival it for sheer natural beauty and abundance of flora and fauna, the incredible geothermal activity in this location makes it unique among American wilderness areas. As well as geysers such as Old Faithful and Steamboat Geyser that blast boiling water hundreds of feet into the air, the park contains many hot springs and mud pots that belch steam and gases from deep below the ground.

Located mostly within the state of Wyoming (3 per cent of its area creeps over the border into Montana and 1 per cent into Idaho), Yellowstone measures 101 kilometers (63 miles) from north to south and 87 kilometers (54 miles) from west to east. Its rugged landscape contains rivers, streams, almost 300 waterfalls and the placid blue waters of Yellowstone Lake. Elsewhere are areas of dense forest and mountain meadows, which contain about 1,700 different species of plant ranging from great conifer trees to rare and delicate flowers around the lakeshore. Within this pristine ecosystem live some of the United States' most endangered species, including the gray wolf and lynx as well as buffalo, mountain lions, grizzly and black bears, moose, deer, elk and mountain goats.

What makes Yellowstone different from many other Alpine landscapes, with which it shares many characteristics, is the fact that most of the park is directly over the Yellowstone Caldera, a 'supervolcano' of devastating power that has the potential to cause a global catastrophe. Although scientists believe that the volcano is already overdue an explosion by tens of thousands

of years there are, at present, few signs of Yellowstone erupting. Nevertheless, relatively close to the surface is a great blister of molten rock, that powers the geothermal features of the area as well as between 1,000 and 2,000 earthquakes that the area experiences every year. No major volcanic activity has been seen above the surface in recent times, but between 2004 and 2006, the floor of the caldera moved upward by 7.6 centimeters (3 in) each year, over three times the rate that has ever before been observed. While this shifting has since slowed, scientists keep a close eye on the region.

Above ground, Yellowstone continues to be one of the United States' most popular national parks, welcoming about two million visitors a year to marvel at the beautiful scenery and fascinating volcanic features. The area has been inhabited by humans for roughly 11,000 years and the park contains historic buildings, visitor centers, and museums where it is possible to view the stone tools and weapons of the ancient tribes who lived here as well as artifacts that document the park's more recent history.

Main image: *A view across Yellowstone National Park's Swan Lake to the cloud-shrouded Electric Peak in the distance. At 3,343 meters (10,969 ft), the mountain is the highest in the Gallatin Range.*

Inset: *With a diameter of 90 meters (295 ft), Yellowstone's Grand Prismatic Spring is the third largest hot spring on the planet, and the largest in the US.*

YOSEMITE NATIONAL PARK

Among the first national parks created in the United States, Yosemite is a breathtaking wilderness of sheer-sided granite peaks, majestic waterfalls, still lakes, groves of giant Sequoia trees and high Alpine meadows. Famous for inspiring the great American photographer Ansel Adams, as well as numerous artists, the park's magnificent vistas form an iconic part of the United States landscape, symbolizing the dramatic scale and untamed beauty of the West.

Located almost in the center of the state of California, Yosemite National Park covers an area of just under 3,100 square kilometers (1,200 sq miles). The dramatic scenery of vertical granite cliffs, deep U-shaped valleys, rounded domes, high lakes and rugged summits was shaped by glaciers over millions of years, and the park boasts abundant streams and rivers that often tumble over the edge of cliffs to form waterfalls. The highest point is Mount Lyell, at 4,000 meters (13,120 ft), though some of the most dramatic peaks, including Half Dome and El Capitan, rear over Yosemite Valley.

Covering the peaks and valleys are a variety of habitats that support a wide range of plants and animals. High chaparral is

characterized by low-growing hardy shrubs and scrub oaks, while elsewhere are stands of Giant Sequoia, which reach heights of 85 meters (280 ft) and measure as much as 8 meters (26 ft) in diameter. The park's oldest is thought to have been a sapling at the time when the Ancient Egyptians began carving tombs in the Valley of the Kings. Yosemite also boasts Alpine meadows and forests of pines and firs, and its habitats are home to a rich diversity of wildlife. Among the larger animals that range the park are black bear, deer, cougar, coyote and the elusive red fox and Western white-tailed jackrabbit. It is also the home of many endangered bird species, such as the Willow flycatcher and California spotted owl.

Unsurprisingly, given its spectacular beauty, Yosemite has long attracted tourists. As early as the mid-19th century more adventurous sightseers and painters had started to arrive, and by the 1880s hotels were springing up to cater to the increasing flood of tourists who were drawn to the pristine wilderness as well as attractions such as the famous Wawona Tree, a Giant Sequoia through which a tunnel was carved.

Fortunately, concerned Californian citizens realized early the effects that unrestricted tourism might have on the area and it was designated a natural preserve by Abraham Lincoln in 1864, later becoming one of America's first national parks.

Today, Yosemite is as popular as ever, and is one of the United States' most fiercely protected wildernesses. A UNESCO World Heritage Site since 1984, it boasts more than 1,300 kilometers (800 miles) of hiking trails and is popular with rock climbers, mountain bikers and many sightseers who just wish to witness one of nature's most splendid landscapes.

Main image: *A view across Yosemite Valley. To the right is the distinctive 1,444-meter (4,737-ft) summit of Half Dome.*

Inset: *Yosemite National Park is famous for its many waterfalls, including the highest, 740-meter (2,425-ft) Yosemite Falls.*

Following pages: *El Capitan (left), towering over the Merced River in Yosemite Valley.*

PICTURE CREDITS

All photographs supplied courtesy of Corbis unless otherwise stated. Individual image credits as follows.

Front cover: Main Image iStock OSTILL, inset images (left to right), iStock djgunner, iStock zxvisual, Bjorn Backe; Papilio, Fridmar Damm, iStock PinkTag.
Back Cover: R. Wallace/Stock Photos, Photolibrary, Michael T. Sedam

I = Insert
Page 1 Michael S. Yamashita, 2 Tom Grill, 6-7 Photosindia, 8-9 Ron Watts, 9 (I) Wolfgang Kaehler, 10-11 Atlantide Phototravel, 10 (I) Image Source, 12-13 TongRo, 14-15 Murat Taner, 15 (I) Robert Essel NYC, 16-17 Francoise Funk-Salami/Keystone, 17 (I) Paul Almasy, 18-19 Jean-Pierre Lescourret, 19 (I) James Emmerson/Robert Harding World Imagery, 20-21 Galen Rowell, 21 (I) Paulo Fridman, 22-23 Torleif Svensson, 24 Deddeda/Design Pics, 25 Yi Lu, 26 Craig Aurness, 27 Arnaud Chicurel/Hemis, 28-29 Yann Arthus-Bertrand, 29 (I) Chris Hellier, 30 Francis G. Mayer, 31 Rex Butcher/JAI, 32-33 ML Sinibaldi, 33 (I) Kevin R. Morris, 34-35 Michele Falzone/JAI, 35 (I) Robert Holmes, 36-37 Ronald Wittek/dpa, 37 (I) Steven Vidler/Eurasia Press, 38-39 Phillip Hayson/Steve Parish Publishing, 38 (I) Photolibrary. 40-41 Photolibrary, 42-43 Tuul/Hemis, 43 (I) John Dakers; Eye Ubiquitous, 44-45 Ali Haider/epa, 44 (I) Ali Haider/epa, 46-47 Carson Ganci/Design Pics, 47 (I) Gavin Hellier/JAI, 48-49 Danielle Gali/JAI, 49 (I) Roman Soumar, 50-51 Jason Hawkes, 51 (I) Gideon Mendel, 52-53 Bob Krist, 52 (I) Ed Darack/Science Faction, 54-55 Ladislav Janicek, 55 (I) Paul A. Souders, 56-57 Robert Harding World Imagery, 57 (I) Kevin Schafer, 58 Jim Zuckerman, 59 Don Hammond/Design Pics, 60-61 Keren Su, 60 (I) Atlantide Phototravel, 62-63 Joseph Sohm/Visions of America, 63 (I) Joseph Sohm/Visions of America, 64-65 Joseph Sohm/Visions of America, 66 Stefen Chow/Aurora Photos, 67 Craig Lovell, 68-69 Buddy Mays, 69 (I) David Muench, 70-71 Redlink, 71 (I) Free Agents Limited, 72 Joseph Sohm/Visions of America, 73 ML Sinibaldi, 74-75 R.CREATION/amanaimages, 75 (I) Kristi J. Black, 76-77 Frans Lanting, 77 (I) Craig Lovell, 78-79 Destinations, 78 (I) Ric Ergenbright, 80-81 Robert Glusic, 81 (I) ImageShop, 82-83 Image Source, 82 (I) Herbert Spichtinger, 84-85 Carl & Ann Purcell, 84 (I) Theo Allofs, 86-87 Stuart Westmorland, 87 (I) Stephen Frink, 88-89 Jose Fuste Raga, 89 (I) Bilderbuch/Design Pics, 90-91 Carson Ganci/Design Pics, 91 (I) Rene Mattes/Hemis, 92-93 Michael T. Sedam, 94-95 Destinations, 95 (I) Frank Lukasseck, 96-97 Ron Chapple, 97 (I) Lester Lefkowitz, 98-99 Walter Bibikow/JAI, 99 (I) Radius Images, 100-101 NASA - digital version copyright/Science Faction, 101 (I) NASA - digital version copyright/Science Faction, 102-103 NASA - digital version copyright/Science Faction, 104 Tibor Bognar, 105 Danny Lehman, 106-107 Frans Lanting, 107 (I) Carlos Moreno/epa, 108-109 Patrick Frilet/Hemism, 109 (I) Rudy Sulgan, 110 Nabil Mounzer/epa, 111 Nabil Mounzer/epa,

112-113 Benjamin Rondel, 113 (I) Jon Arnold/JAI, 152-153 James Montgomery/JAI, 153 (I) Imagemore Co., Ltd., 114-115 James Montgomery/JAI, 115 (I) Imagemore Co., Ltd., 116 Frédéric Soltan/Sygma, 117 Ivan Vdovin/JAI, 119 (I) Kazuyoshi Nomachi, 120-121 Gavin Hellier/JAI, 121 (I) Blaine Harrington III, 122 Jeff Albertson, 123 Jose Fuste Raga, 124-125 Takashi Katahira/amanaimages, 124 (I) Tim Davis, 126-127 Casa Productions, 127 (I) Herwarth Voigtmann, 128-129 Sandro Vannini, 129 (I) Sergio Pitamitz, 130-131 Peter M. Wilson, 131 (I) Walter Bibikow/JAI, 132-133 Peter Adams, 133 (I) Michele Westmorland, 134-135 Charles & Josette Lenars, 135 (I) Charles & Josette Lenars, 136-137 Jane Sweeney/JAI, 137 (I) Marc Dozier/Hemis, 138-139 Image Source, 138 (I) Paul Souders, 140-141 Ray Juno, 141 (I) David Muench, 142 Fred Hirschmann/Science Faction, 143 Fred Hirschmann/Science Faction, 144-145 Stocktrek Images/Infocus Imagery, 146-147 Jeff Foott/Science Faction, 147 (I) Frank Lukasseck, 148-149 Hasse Schröder/Naturbild, 148 (I) Tommy Olofsson/Nordicphotos, 150-151 Jorge Ferrari/epa, 151 (I) Jumana El Heloueh, 152-153 Danny Lehman, 153 (I) Jane Sweeney/JAI, 154-155 Gavin Hellier/Robert Harding World Imagery, 155 (I) Mike Theiss/Ultimate Chase, 156 O. Alamany & E. Vicens, 157 Robert Landau, 158 Murat Taner, 159 Scott Stulberg, 160-161 Atlantide Phototravel, 161 (I) Sylvain Sonnet, 162-163 Rob Howard, 163 (I) Antonio Broto/EFE, 164-165 Image Source, 166-167 Philippe Body/Hemis, 167 (I) Paul Hardy, 168-169 Michael Freeman, 169 (I) Andrew McConnell/Robert Harding World Imagery, 170-171 Philip James Corwin, 171 (I) Charles Mauzy, 172-173 Owaki – Kulla, 172 (I) Bettmann, 174 Mohamed Messara/epa, 175 Jamal Nasrallah/epa, 176-177 Werner H. Mueller, 177 (I) Frank Krahmer, 178-179 Sylvain Sonnet, 179 (I) David Clapp/Arcaid, 180-181 O. Alamany & E. Vicens, 180 (I) W. Perry Conway, 182 Zhu Huanan(JIANGSU)/XinHua/Xinhua Press, 183 Jay Pasachoff/Science Faction, 184-185 John Harper, 184 (I) Tom Grill, 186-187 Bilderbuch/Design Pics, 187 (I) Jason Hawkes, 188-189 Paul Prince/LOOP IMAGES/Loop Images, 190-191 NASA, 190 (I) Bettmann, 192-193 R. Wallace/Stock Photos, 192 (I) L. Clarke, 194-195 Gallo Images, 195 (I) Bob Krist, 196-197 Top Photo Corporation, 197 (I) Jose Fuste Raga, 198 Michael Busselle, 199 Brian A. Vikander, 200-201 Angelo Hornak, 201 (I) Charles & Josette Lenars, 202-203 Imagemore Co., Ltd., 203 (I) Imagemore Co., Ltd., 204-205 Atlantide Phototravel, 205 (I) Radius Images, 206 John Noble, 207 Blaine Harrington III, 208-209 Atlantide Phototravel, 209 (I) Christian Kober/Robert Harding World Imagery, 210-211 Mark Karrass, 211 (I) Paul A. Souders, 212-213 Dave Bartruff, 212 (I) Sandro Vannini, 214-215 Douglas Schwartz, 214 (I) Massimo Listri, 216 Patrick Ward, 217 Atlantide Phototravel, 218-219 Eric and David Hosking, 219 (I) Frank Lukasseck, 220-221 James Randklev, 221 (I) Bill Ross, 222-223 Michele Falzone/JAI

Project Managed by BlueRed Press Ltd.